LOCOMOTION PAPERS

CW00434465

The Kingsbridge Branch

The Primrose Line

by
Ken Williams and Dermot Reynolds

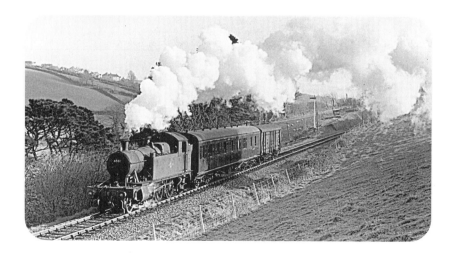

THE OAKWOOD PRESS

© Oakwood Press, Ken Williams and Dermot Reynolds 1997

British Library Cataloguing in Publication Data
A Record for this book is available from the British Library
ISBN 0 85361 493 8

Typeset by Oakwood Graphics.
Repro by Ford Graphics, Ringwood, Hants.
Printed by Alpha Print (Oxford) Ltd, Witney, Oxon.

First published by the Oxford Publishing Co. 1977
Second revised edition 1997

The Dartmouth coach and carriages meeting a train hauled by a 'Metro' tank at Kingsbridge station, *c.* 1900.   *Cookworthy Museum*

Front Cover: 2-6-2T No. 5558 runs-round at the Brent end of Kingsbridge station, 15th July, 1958.   *R.C. Riley*

Title Page: '45XX' class 2-6-2T No. 4561 is seen on the 4.15 pm from Kingsbridge heading towards Sorley with Kingsbridge's fixed distant signal in the background, 5th March, 1960.   *P.W. Gray*

Published by
The Oakwood Press
P.O. Box 122, Headington, Oxford OX3 8LU

Contents

Kingsbridge station just prior to opening, October 1893.   *Cookworthy Museum*

R.E. Toop

No. 5558 runs towards the stock for the Kingsbridge branch at Brent on 5th August, 1958.

Preface to Second Edition

It is now 20 years since the first edition was published by the Oxford Publishing Co. and 18 years since *The Kingsbridge Branch* was last in print. The intervening years have seen a continuing interest in the branch and a growing demand for detailed historic and photographic information; on this basis it was decided to publish a new edition with the inclusion of many new and hitherto unpublished photographs. Chapter Ten, The Epilogue, has been updated taking into account developments over the last 20 years.

It is hoped this reprinted work will once again revive memories for those who knew the branch as a working railway, and, to those who have discovered the area in more recent times after closure of the branch, provide a graphic story of what was surely one of the most scenically beautiful branch lines in the country.

Dermot Reynolds
February 1997

Foreword to First Edition

This is a book about railways and about part of Devonshire I know well. My enthusiasms for both go back to early childhood, and were very much brought together during my time as Divisional Manager of British Railways Plymouth Division in 1963-64.

The railways have been a force in the transport life of this country for over 150 years; their continuing ability to serve the nation has been much linked with their success in meeting changing circumstances with new ideas and by encouraging forward looking developments.

In looking ahead to the future we must, however, always be ready to learn from the past. That is what this book sets out to do. Here we have the story of the evolution of public transport in the South Hams area of Devon; we see the role which the railway played in that evolution; and we have a glimpse of that famous and successful pioneering company at work - the Great Western Railway.

The authors - and their love of the GWR and all it stood for comes through strongly in the book - have brought the facts together in a wider setting of local history, geography and anecdote.

As one who feels 'at home' in Devon; as a 'Western' man by upbringing and a railwayman of some 35 years standing, I commend this book to you. I am sure you will enjoy it.

David Pattisson
Chief Administration Officer
British Railways Board
London NW1
April 1977

No. 4568 is seen at Avonwick on 30th August, 1956 on the 2.10 pm to Brent. *M. Hale*

No. 5573 with the 12.00 pm to Kingsbridge waits to pass an up goods at Gara Bridge on 2nd August, 1960. *R.E. Toop*

Introduction

This book sets out to recount not merely the story of the Kingsbridge branch - the railway - but the story of an era, the historical background of the area, the very early yet abortive plans, the personal accounts of both passengers and staff, the maintenance of an integrated transport system of which the railway naturally played the key role, and finally its inevitable 'planned' demise.

The authors have endeavoured to recall what life was like on 'the railway' - through the memories of the men for whom it was their life; this will, we trust, act as a vivid nostalgic reminder to the many thousands of people who throughout nearly seventy years of operation, experienced the unique rural charm of this branch line.

Natural evidence of the line's very existence disappears more year by year, as more cuttings are filled in and more embankments are removed, to be reclaimed by their new owners. Much detailed physical information has been included, in the form of maps, diagrams, drawings, and photographs, for those wishing to 'model' and preserve - albeit in miniature form - the Kingsbridge Branch. The bibliographical index will act as a further source of reference, should this be required.

Acknowledgement has been given to the many people who have contributed towards the collection of material for this book in order to provide the basis of a manuscript. It is the authors' sincere wish that their final collated result will give pleasure and provide a memorable and historic tribute to the Kingsbridge branch.

Ken Williams
Dermot Reynolds

Auto Coach No. 231
Didcot
September 1976

Loddiswell station looking towards Brent, Summer 1956.   *Dermot Reynolds Collection*

7

Fore Street, Kingsbridge from an old picture postcard. *Ken Williams Collection*

Fruit Boats at Dates Yard, Kingsbridge in the mid-1890s. *Ken Williams Collection*

Chapter One

Glorious Devon

Kingsbridge For Salcombe

'Glorious Devon' is the title of a book published by the Great Western Railway in 1928 which went into eight editions; written by S.P.B. Mais it is still a much sought after book today.

A part of this most beautiful county is known as the South Hams and it is this area with which this book is concerned.

Devon has been a seafaring county for centuries as well as providing food and minerals for our nation and this is certainly true of the South Hams. This area is bounded in the east by the River Dart, the Totnes to Plymouth railway line to the north and the River Yealm in the west, with the sea to the south.

The word 'Ham' is Anglo-Saxon meaning 'flat low lying water meadow and enclosed pasture.' Much of Saxon origin remains to remind us today of the past. Perhaps the most obvious connections are in the place names of the towns, villages and hamlets. Those place names ending in -TON being Saxon for homestead (Yealmpton), -LEIGH means wooded glade (Woodleigh), -WELL indicates a Holy spring (Loddiswell), -BOROUGH shows that this was once a fortified area (Malborough), -FORD is obvious as a river or valley crossing place (Diptford) and -WICK means a hamlet or district (Avonwick). The coastal features also have Saxon names, -BOLT meaning arrow, -START or STORT a tail, and -PRAWLE a look out. Indeed the name Kingsbridge is Saxon in origin. It is believed the King referred to was a 'Saxon' and the 'Bridge' was a causeway over the upper estuary.

Kingsbridge is mentioned in an Anglo-Saxon document of 962 when King Edgar granted some estates to a lord who later gave them to the monks at Buckfast. With the increase of agriculture, other industries sprang up and the demand for other skills arose. Because of the demand for the various uses of leather, the curing of meat, fish and salt was required and, as a result, salt was manufactured from brine at Bigbury and fishing became an occupation - fresh water at Loddiswell, salt water at Kingsbridge. Life was comparatively easy with little hostility.

In 1066 William the Conqueror landed at Hastings and this of course was the last successful invasion of our shores by an enemy. King William's supporters were soon being rewarded for their support and loyalty whilst the Anglo-Saxons were dispossessed of their lands. Despite the Norman wealth and influence, however, little remains today to remind us of their occupation, save the local churches such as Kingsbridge, Loddiswell and Salcombe.

With the advent of the Normans life settled down to a more or less regular pattern throughout the rest of the country. In the middle ages (15/16th centuries) a rapid interest in the church developed under the influence of the monks at Buckfast, leading to the building of many churches. This influence vanished at the Dissolution, but the thriving mills set up by the monks

High tide at Kingsbridge *c.* 1912.   *Ken Williams Collection*

The Quay, Kingsbridge in the 1930s.   *Ken Williams Collection*

remained. It is recorded that the export of woollen cloth to Florence in Italy began at this time.

As one can imagine, especially if one examines the coast at Bigbury, Thurlestone, and Salcombe, the terrain was ideal for pirates to lay up. Dartmouth was the principal base and ships from Spain, Giron, France, Algeria and Morocco plied their piratical trade right up to the end of the 17th century - the Kingsbridge/Salcombe estuary being ideal for hiding out. The piracy of the 17th century gave way to smuggling in the 18th century and smuggling tales are legend.

The Cromwellian upheaval in the 17th century left its mark within the area. Bitter battles were fought, but the locals had no real wish to be involved. The Puritans wrought havoc in the beautiful houses and churches of the South Hams stripping such things as precious gems and pictures and despoiling the buildings, especially churches. Modbury church is said to have been used as a stable.

The demand for food ensured the development of agriculture and the Red Devon breed of cow prospered. Kingsbridge became the focal point for the South Hams and its port was busy with sailing schooners loading wool, tools, ropes and building materials - stone and slate. In addition there was cider and beer brewing, textile mills and flour mills. With this movement of ships it was inevitable that shipbuilding and the associated maintenance facilities would be set up.

The Kingsbridge estuary was, in the later part of the 18th century, thronged with ships of all types and sizes waiting to discharge their cargoes of cocoa, coffee, tobacco, sugar, spices, ginger, timber, cotton, grain, wines, rubber, silk and so on - almost a limitless manifest of cargoes.

The South Hams not only built ships but also the men folk provided part of the essential ships' companies. The fruit trade from distant lands led to the building of fruit clippers, fast easily maintained vessels, mainly at Kingsbridge in the yards of Messrs Dates (now part of the car park of the Crabshell Inn). The yard later turned to trawlers and fishing craft but closed at the turn of the century although, ironically, small pleasure craft are still built in the old Kingsbridge station goods shed. At Salcombe, the yards gave the town an air of importance with the sounds of shipwright's craft from sunrise to sunset. Now the only work is in pleasure craft at Salcombe, whilst cargo ships ceased to call many decades ago. The vast forests in the area provided much of the timber for the various yards.

Because of the shipbuilding industry other skills were required, not least the manufacture of ropes and the various cutting tools required by the yards. The rope walk at Kingsbridge is now commemorated in name only.

Movement within the South Hams during this early history was very restricted and people relied on foot or horse for moving about. The first coach service began in 1824 operated by Robert Foale of Kingsbridge, departing from the King's Arms. With the opening of the South Devon Railway in 1848, these coaches met trains at Kingsbridge Road station (Wrangaton). A steamer service began in the 1860s operated by the Kingsbridge Packet Company running twice weekly to Plymouth calling at Salcombe. Later, a daily coach service ran between Dartmouth and Kingsbridge (Anchor Hotel) connecting with the Kingswear trains running three times a day.

However, little change in travelling habits occurred until the eventual arrival of the railway (in 1893) in Kingsbridge; and with the introduction of the motor bus (1909), by the GWR, moving from one place to another became easier. The steamer service to Plymouth continued to run into the 20th century and also the Kingsbridge-Salcombe service, taken over by the Great Western in 1929. With the arrival of the railway, the South Hams became attractive to the holiday maker and the tourist industry began to develop.

Before moving on with our story mention must be made of William Cookworthy, possibly Kingsbridge's most famous citizen. Born in Kingsbridge on 12th April, 1705 the son of a weaver, William was a keen scholar and trained in chemistry. When visiting Cornwall in 1748, Cookworthy discovered china clay at Tregonning Hill; this finding led to Cookworthy launching out in the porcelain industry. However, Cookworthy sold out his patent and never made much money from his discovery; he was a devout Quaker and had no interest in acquiring wealth.

The fruits of his researches and discovery passed to the Staffordshire pottery industry, but it is thanks to Cookworthy that we have the beautiful porcelain from years past to grace our homes. Cookworthy is remembered to this day in Kingsbridge by the Cookworthy Museum. This is a charming rural museum, full of interesting relics of the history and passage of time in the South Hams.

We have now briefly traced the development of the South Hams and with only minor changes taking place the community prospered, but without much outside influence. The arrival of the railway changed all that and even today the area is continually changing, but to many people not for the better. The improvement of roads and the new motorways bring car owners, trailing caravans and boats to the narrow South Devon lanes in increasing numbers. Salcombe, Thurlestone, Bigbury and Slapton are all great 'holiday haunts' and yet the historian and archaeologist can still find much of great interest; there are still quite peaceful places to be found.

Truly 'Glorious Devon'.

Fore Street and The King's Arms, Kingsbridge from an old picture postcard.
Ken Williams Collection

Chapter Two

The Beginning - A False Start

On the 1st May, 1844 the Bristol and Exeter Railway was completed and the main line from London to Exeter - GWR to Bristol - was opened. This was the longest line in the land at that time, 194 miles from Paddington via Bristol to Exeter.

The Royal Assent was given to the South Devon Railway Company on 4th July, 1844 to construct a line to Plymouth as an extension to the Bristol and Exeter Railway. The GWR even at that early stage kept in close contact with all developments in the West Country, subscribing £150,000 to the project. The line was opened to Teignmouth on 30th May, 1846; to Newton Abbot on 30th December, 1846*; to Totnes by 20th July, 1847; to Laira Green on 5th May, 1848, and finally to Plymouth on 2nd April, 1849. The South Devon Railway hired its motive power from the GWR until 1851 and thereafter from contractors, at no time could it be regarded as a completely independent company. Eleven of its Directors out of a Board of 21 were nominated by other companies.

When Isambard Kingdom Brunel surveyed the Exeter to Plymouth section in 1836, the motive power available at that time was incapable of hauling the stock over the steep gradients of the shorter route round the southern edge of Dartmoor. The South Devon Railway was certainly in favour of linking centres of population on a western route and as a result an alternative route was suggested via Torquay, over the Dart estuary to Dartmouth, thence via the coast to Torcross and into the South Hams, skirting Kingsbridge, to Modbury and finally to Plymouth. Ironically the motive power of the period began to show its capabilities for hill climbing at the time when route decisions were being taken, and the coastal route was abandoned in favour of the route built via Newton Abbot and Totnes. In retrospect, should the coastal route have been chosen, it is more likely that Kingsbridge would still have a rail connection today. It is interesting to note that the only intermediate station actually completed for the opening on 5th May, 1848 was Wrangaton which was re-named Kingsbridge Road early in 1849 as a result of a 'memorial' to Kingsbridge - but renamed back to Wrangaton in 1895 after the opening of the Kingsbridge branch.

With all the rapid development of the early 19th century and the more stable life of that period certain people in the South Hams, having heard and read of the development of railways in England, decided that Kingsbridge should also have its own railway. Accordingly in the 1850s plans were discussed at meetings held to propose such a railway.

At the Town Hall, Kingsbridge on 22nd October, 1854, Lord Courtney took the chair and proposed a railway from Churston via Dartmouth and Slapton to Kingsbridge. There was enthusiasm for this scheme but unfortunately no money and this proposal died a quick death.

The early 1860s saw more proposals resulting in plans being laid before

---

* 30th according to SDR and GWR records, although recently the 31st has been suggested as the correct date.

Parliament in 1863 for a line leaving the South Devon Railway at Brent on the west side and curving down to join the River Avon at Avonwick and into Kingsbridge.

At a meeting in January 1864, held at Kingsbridge, a company was floated with a capital of £130,000 in £10 shares. Two brothers from Loddiswell immediately subscribed £2,000, pointing out that this was an investment not a donation, to fire the enthusiasm for other local folk to do likewise. The meeting finally raised or promised £6,000. Subsequently an Act of Parliament was applied for by the Kingsbridge and Salcombe Railway and finally granted by 27 & 28 Vict. cap. 287 29th July, 1864. 'To construct a line from South Brent on the South Devon Railway to Kingsbridge. Length 12¼ miles.' Capital was £130,000 in £10 shares and £43,000 on loan - arrangements with the South Devon Railway for hire of motive power were planned.

By 29 & 30 Vict. cap. 264 23rd July, 1866 the company was authorised to make several deviations to raise new capital to the extent of £60,000 in shares, £17,000 on loan. Work commenced on 24th June, 1867 and the contractor was a Mr Chambers.

There is a copy (in BR Archives) of a letter from the company to the South Devon Railway (SDR) as follows:

Dear Sir,
    Our Contractor has as you are probably aware commenced the works on this line.
    A suggestion has recently been made with reference to a point, which as it is of immediate importance to us, I hasten to bring before your Company.
    That is, that your concurrence should be obtained to the construction of this branch on the narrow gauge.
    Considering the impending arrangement between the Lon: & South West: narrow gauge and the several broad gauge systems of the West (the bill for which, though withdrawn for this year is to be reintroduced next session) and the fact that the Bristol & Exeter Company are adopting the mixed gauge, in view of this arrangement, it does seem to my Company to be imposing a needless burden upon us to compel us to construct our little line - the trains or carriages from which will never run through over your main line - upon the broad gauge, at a considerable additional expense, and with no benefit to either party. etc. etc.
Yours faithfully,
(Signature not known.)

Obviously the SDR was pressurising the Kingsbridge company.

It was not long before a ceremony was arranged by the Directors for the laying of the foundation stone of the first bridge over the Avon. By all accounts this was an excuse for the whole area to join in and have a 'fling'. Kingsbridge was decorated with flags and bunting and at the bridge site a tent was erected and the contractor entertained the Directors to lunch. Mrs Fortesque, wife of the Chairman, performed the ceremony during which a bottle containing coins of the realm was deposited under the foundation stone.

There appeared a notice in the *Western Morning News* dated 26th August, 1867 as follows:

The Kingsbridge Railway. The Foundation stone of the first bridge of this railway over the River Avon, about two miles above Loddiswell, will be laid on Saturday afternoon by Mrs Fortesque, the lady of Mr W.B. Fortesque Chairman of the Directors. A large tent is being erected on the picturesque grounds near the river at Topsham for the interesting occasion, and a luncheon will be provided for the directors and officers of the company by Mr Charles Chambers, the Contractor.

The balance sheet for 1867 showed the following. Income came from receipts on calls £4,188, interest and loans bringing up the amount to £5,920.

Expenditure

Preliminary and Parliamentary		£4,401
Land and compensation		540
Salaries and office expenses		178
Cash at Bank		800
	(rounded)	£5,920

There were five Directors each with a minimum qualification of £100. They were: Wm B. Fortesque (Chairman); Mr Oaten, Torquay; The Rt Hon. Earl Devon, Powderham Castle, Exeter; W. John Elliot, Kingsbridge; Wm Roope Ilbert, Kingsbridge; the Surveyor being Mr J. Drew Jnr - Powderham Castle. The registered office was 7, Westminster Chambers, Victoria Street, Westminster.

By the end of September 1868 the borrowing powers were resorted to - to the tune of £43,000 at 5 per cent. The balance sheet for that year:

Received

Share capital on Deposit	£13,939	
Shares fully paid up	20	
	13,959	
Interest	85	
	£14,044	£14,044
Expenses to 31st December, 1867		£7,962
Land purchased—compensation and cost		1,390
Engineering		300
Works		3,016
Salaries and office expenses including rent, clerks		147
Travel expenses		39
Law expenses		34
Cash at bank		1,156
		£14,044

A degree of pessimism crept into the company reports of 1869, and it was resolved at a special meeting in September to issue the debentures under the Act of 1864 'and the Directors looking to the market improvement in this class of security thought there would be no difficulty in placing them, and trusted that a considerable amount would be taken by the shareholders to whom they would be offered', as quoted in *Bradshaw's Railway Manual* 1870. The total amount proposed to be issued under the powers of the Act of 1864 was £43,000 and, 'as the shareholders have been previously reminded, they bear the guarantee of the South Devon Railway for the due payment of the interest at the rate of 5 per cent per annum.' This was a vain endeavour to instill certain confidence into a rapidly declining project by illustrating to the shareholders that interest was supported by the owners of the main line - but what was not realised locally at the time was that the SDR was really in no position to give any major support to a venture on such an unsound basis.

Early in 1871 the inevitable situation arose; notice was issued to the effect that the company was applying to the Board of Trade for the abandonment of the undertaking.

However, there is a copy of a report dated 11th August, 1874 to the Kingsbridge company, presumably by the Engineer of the SDR, which reads as follows:

As requested I yesterday went over the line of the Kingsbridge Railway - as shown on that Company's plans of 1873.

The proposed line commences at the turnpike gate to the south side of Kingsbridge and ascends by a gradient of 1 in 55 to the summit and passing under the Plymouth Turnpike road by a tunnel 450 yards in length, descends by a gradient of 1 in 56 to near Loddiswell Bridge - it then follows the course of the River Avon to near Topsham Bridge - from this point a length of about one mile has been fenced in and the line partially formed - from thence onward to half mile above Gara Bridge nothing has been done except to fence in about six chains of line (now proposed to be abandoned for an improved course). From 7 miles 5 furlongs to 9 miles the line is fenced and partially constructed, but from that point to the junction at Brent nothing whatever has been done. The total length of the proposed line is 12¼ miles and of this only 2 miles and 30 chains have been commenced and this consists chiefly of surface forming construction from the cutting at the end of each portion of the work commenced - a small cutting below Bickham Bridge about 10 feet deep and 8 chains in length is completed - the formation width is 15 feet. A few stones for bottom ballast are laid for about 1 chain in length in this cutting.

The fencing is composed of the ordinary posts and wires.

The only works of note constructed are an arch over the line at Bickham Bridge but without ramps or road approaches and close by it a small cattle bridge of 6 feet span. A stone bridge of two segmented arches each 25 ft span has been constructed over the river near Bickham Bridge - and a skew stone bridge of 2 segmented arches each of 20 ft square span over the River at Topsham Bridge. A level crossing lodge has also been constructed at this latter place - the masonry in the Bridges is slight and rough in character.

In November 1864 a further Act was laid before Parliament called 'The South Hams (Devon) Railway' for the 1865 session. This railway was to run from the SDR, passing through Ridgeway, Yealmpton, Modbury, Aveton Gifford, Churchstow into Kingsbridge and then out along the coast to Dartmouth, following the proposed 1854 route.

During this period a local, under the pen name 'Townsman', tried to rally an 'Anti-Railway' group to thwart all these proposals. Perhaps as the railway was delayed so long, it achieved some success.

A further proposal in November 1865 led to another Act being laid before Parliament called 'The Kingsbridge Railway Deviation and Extension to Salcombe'. This proposal was for a line leaving the east side of Brent (Deviation

2) along the Avon Valley through South Loddiswell into Kingsbridge (Deviation 1) and then extended along the estuary to Salcombe.

Neither of these schemes became reality and all thoughts of a local railway vanished, although considerable correspondence took place in the *Kingsbridge Gazette*.

A further Act in 1872 sought to establish a railway but nothing came of this plan. Again in 1875 a narrow gauge line (believed 3 ft 6 in.) was proposed, but interest soon petered out.

On 1st February, 1876 the South Devon Railway amalgamated with the Great Western Railway. This naturally offered a major opportunity for a revival of the project. The GWR was eager to link with its main line as many centres of population as possible, to provide a useful traffic supplement to this line and ensure comprehensive coverage of an area hitherto without this means of communication.

It was not until 24th July, 1882 that the Kingsbridge & Salcombe Railway was incorporated by Act of Parliament to construct a railway from Brent station on the Great Western main line to Kingsbridge and Salcombe.

This Act of 1882 incorporated the proposals of the 1863 and 1866 Acts and repealed the earlier Acts. But the line would still continue out to Salcombe, terminating at Ibberstone Point with road access from the King's Arms quay, a distance of 16 miles. The Act was amended to take the terminus nearer to Salcombe, the station to be sited just to the east of the parish church.

A period of five years was allowed for the completion - which later proved rather optimistic to say the least. Working arrangements were agreed with the GWR with regard to stock, traffic and motive power. The authorised capital was £160,000 in £10 shares with powers to divide into preferred and deferred half shares - borrowing powers of up to £53,000 were also agreed.

The Directors of the company were:

Colonel Walker	-	Chairman
The Rt Hon. Earl of Devon*	-	Powderham Castle
Wm Roope llbert JP*	-	Bowringsleigh, Kingsbridge
Richard Basset	-	Highclere, near Newbury
Alexander Hubbard	-	Derwentwater House, Acton, London
Edwin Fox	-	Kingsbridge
Benjamin Lake	-	Kingsbridge
F.W. Fox CE	-	The Engineer, London
Booty and Baycliffe	-	Company Solicitors

Constitution: Directors maximum 7, minimum 3, Quorum 5 x 2. Qualification 25 shares. *Directors of the original company.

The offices of the company were at 17, Great George Street, Westminster, and at a Board meeting on 21st February, 1883 the above named were elected Directors, whilst a Richard John Palmer was appointed to act as Secretary.

At this meeting the Prospectus of the company was approved and leave given for its issue and a tender for constructing the railway received from a firm - Messrs Lidstone - was approved in principle and subject to a letter from the company solicitors. Further approval was given for the acquisition of a suitable company seal.

With the issuing of the Prospectus it was hoped that money would flood in and the work be put in hand. However, on 18th July, Mr Fox advised the Board that only £1,500 in shares had been applied for. Mr Fox further disclosed that he had approached several other contractors and interest had been shown, subject to certain guarantees. An approach had been made to the Great Western for an advance of £50,000 but the GWR had declined. Possibly the GWR hoped for an early take over but declined any financial help and held this position until at least the end of January 1884. The company's bankers - The Devon and Cornwall Bank - agreed to renew a promissory note for £8,000 for a period of six months.

During the later part of 1883 a Mr Wilson is mentioned as being a contractor for the line, but no definite proposals were received.

An undertaking was given by the Board on 28th January, 1884 to Mr Wilson's agents that there were no negotiations pending or being entered into with any party for the next fortnight and the company requested a definite and final answer by the 16th February. The Board were advised at this meeting that Messrs Lidstone's had withdrawn their offer. It would appear that Mr Wilson was not forthcoming with any proposals, for in the Board Minutes of 25th February, 1884 a resolution was passed that Mr Wilson be pressed for an answer.

During this period the Earl of Devon had a meeting with the GWR but met with no success in the raising of capital for the company.

At the 31st July, 1884 Board meeting, the Earl of Devon and Mr Lake tendered their resignations from the Board; however at this time considerable interest was being shown by various contractors. The Board decided to approach the GWR to establish if the latter would be prepared to operate the line if it were opened in sections rather than wait until completion of the whole line.

The Board met on 29th April, 1885 and below are the Minutes of the meeting:

Secretary reported that the Great Western Company had expressed their willingness to meet the wishes of the Directors to work the Line should it be completed in sections.

Mr Baycliffe reported that the sum of £7,000 in cash would be required to rescind the Contract for 25,000 shares in the Company.

The proposal made by Mr G. Barclay Bruce was read by Mr Lidstone and considered, and it was resolved that the proposal be and is hereby accepted as the basis for a Contract subject to the following stipulations viz:

(1) That in the event of the cost of the land exceeding the limit of £8,000 the contract shall not necessarily be (? abandoned) but shall be determinable by either party without any claim on the part of the Contractor for consequential damage.

(2) That the Great Western Company accept the modifications required by the Contractor.

(3) That all claims of the old Company and for Engineering Law and Administration up to and during construction including all preliminary expenses are settled and provided for to the Contractor's satisfaction and so as to release the Company.

(4) That the Contractor undertakes all responsibility in respect of the Parliamentary deposits including all arrears of interest and relieves the Directors at present liable.

(5) That the acceptance of the proposal in conditional on the completion of a formal Contract within one month from this date failing which the Directors reserve the right to cancel or modify this resolution.

(6) That the Secretary forthwith transmits a copy of this resolution to Mr Bruce.

The resignations of the Earl of Devon and Mr Lake were accepted.

Various Contractors came and went over the ensuing months. However, the GWR had expressed an interest in purchasing the Act of 1882.

At a meeting of the GWR Board held on the 28th October, 1885 the General Manager explained the position of matters with respect to the Kingsbridge Railway and he submitted a letter from Messrs Booty and Bayliffe, the solicitors to the latter company, dated 27th October, stating that, 'if within a fortnight the Promoters have not made such arrangements as will ensure the Line being forthwith commenced and carried on to completion, in accordance with the terms of the proposed Agreement with the Great Western Company, they will be prepared to hand over the Undertaking to the latter, so that they may themselves construct the line.'

The GWR Board took the bold step of accepting this proposal and Mr Grierson the General Manager was authorised 'in the event of the Promoters failing to satisfy him within the time specified of their ability to carry out the arrangements referred to, to negotiate with them for the transfer of their powers to nominees of this Company on the best terms he can arrange.'

When the GWR Board met on 18th November, 1886, the General Manager submitted a letter which he had received from Messrs Booty and Bayliffe stating that, 'in consequence of the Contractors, on whom the Promoters of the Kingsbridge Railway relied, having declined to proceed further in the business, the Promoters are not at the present time able to arrange for the construction of the Line, and are prepared to carry out the alternative proposal made by the Great Western Company viz: that the Company should take over the powers of the Kingsbridge and Salcombe Company upon payment of the sum of £8,000, to include every expense, the land and works belonging to the old Company as well as all plans, deeds and documents. The offer being subject to an indemnity being given against all claim or claims; to an arrangement with the land owners with regard to the land; and to a release from Lord Devon as to the Line beyond Kingsbridge.'

By the 3rd August, 1887 the GWR Board met and reported as follows under minute No 38:

In reference to Minute No. 26 of the meeting of the Board held on the 18th November last, the General Manager submitted a letter dated 29th ultimo, from Messrs Booty and Bayliffe, the Solicitors of the Kingsbridge and Salcombe Railway stating that an Act for an extension of the powers for the purchase of the land and the construction of the works had been obtained this session and offering to dispose of such powers, with the land and works belonging to the original Kingsbridge Company, which they have agreed to acquire, for the sum of £10,000.

The letter explains the position of the negotiations for the acquisition of the remainder of the land required, from which it appears that only in a few cases had any definite arrangements been concluded.

The General Manager was instructed to inform Messrs Booty and Bayliffe that the conditions of the offer made by the Board on 6th August, 1885 had not been complied with, 'and that they are not therefore prepared to negotiate for the acquisition of the powers from the Kingsbridge and Salcombe Company until more definite arrangements have been made with the landowners for the acquisition of the necessary land'.

This meeting continued on the 11th August when Mr Grierson reported under Minute No. 19 that, 'in consequence of the delay on the part of the Kingsbridge Railway Company in carrying out the conditions on which negotiations for taking over their powers and property were contingent, which is stated to have arisen from difficulty in arranging with the landowners, he had informed them that the negotiations with this Company (GWR) were to be considered at an end and the alternative offer made in 1885 withdrawn.'

The offer of Messrs Booty and Bayliffe referred to in the before mentioned Minute having been declined, it had been intimated that the Kingsbridge Company would be willing to dispose of its powers etc. for a less sum than £10,000.

Mr Grierson was therefore authorised 'to conclude an arrangement for the payment of a sum not exceeding £9,000 subject to arrangements being made to the satisfaction of the Great Western Company with the landowners upon the Kingsbridge Line, both as to the price to be paid for and as to the accommodation work to be provided in respect of such land, the reasonable expenses of the negotiations incurred with their previous consent and of any plans and agreements in connection therewith to be borne by this Company.'

Progress was extremely slow to the extent that work came more or less to a standstill in 1886; however an Act was granted on 8th August, 1887 to extend the time for completion of works until 24th July, 1890. There was still a financial uncertainty as Kingsbridge at this time was relatively prosperous from its small but lucrative shipbuilding business and river trading by its navigable estuary - the latter probably a major factor in the failure of previous schemes, whilst established marine traders feared the competition from the railway.

At a time when financial disaster for the 'old' company seemed inevitable the Kingsbridge & Salcombe Board met on 8th December, 1887 to hear the company Solicitor read the Agreement drawn up by the Solicitor to the Great Western Railway for the purchase of the company. It was then resolved that the same be approved and confirmed subject to the additions suggested by the Solicitor.

On 19th December, 1887 the Board met and the Secretary was authorised to seal the Agreement as amended by the Board provided the same contained no alterations inserted by the Great Western Railway Company of a nature unfavourable to the interests of the Kingsbridge Railway, and subject to the approval of the Solicitor.

By 2nd February, 1888 the Secretary reported that the Seal of the company had been affixed to the Agreement with the Great Western Railway Company.

To continue our narrative it is perhaps better for the reader to absorb the detail of the relative GWR Board Minutes:

21st December, 1887
Minute 49. In reference to Minute No. 19 of the meeting held on the 11th August last, the Chairman reported that he had had an interview with some of the Directors of the Kingsbridge and Salcombe Railway Company who requested the desirability of proceeding at once with the construction of the Line between South Brent and Kingsbridge.

The Officers of this Company have also met representatives of the Kingsbridge Company and arranged the terms of the Agreement for the taking over of the powers of the Kingsbridge and Salcombe Railway Company and the appointment of a Board solely composed of Great Western Directors.

The amount to be paid for the costs incurred by the Promoters (including the purchase of the land acquired from the old Company viz: - £3,500) is £9,000 which covers also the costs of the negotiations for the land purchased.

The arrangement was approved and it was resolved that the Chairman, Deputy Chairman, Mr Basset and Mr Michell be requested to act as Directors of the Kingsbridge Company, in conjunction with Sir Massey Lopes and Mr Hubbard who had already been nominated as such, but who, for reasons stated, had not yet taken their seats on the Board:

The Agreement provides for the taking over by this Company at their market value of the Consols forming the deposit for the Kingsbridge and Salcombe Bill of 1882, provision having been inserted in this Company's Bill (No. 1) for the release of the deposit upon the powers of the Company being vested in the Great Western Company.

8th March, 1888
Minute 23. In reference to Minute 49 of the meeting of the Board held on the 21st December last, the Chairman reported that, from inquiries he had made, he found that the Agreement for the purchase of the land upon the Kingsbridge Line were so far advanced as to admit of steps being taken for qualifying the Great Western representatives upon the Kingsbridge Board, in substitution for the present Directors, and for so obtaining the control of the undertaking.

This course was approved and the necessary arrangements were authorised.

21st March, 1888
Minute 10. In reference to Minute No 23 of the Meeting of the Board held on the 8th instant, Sir Daniel Gooch, Sir Alexander Hood, Mr Basset, Mr Hubbard, Sir Massey Lopes and Mr Michell were requested to execute the Subscription Contract with the Kingsbridge and Salcombe Railway Company to the extent of £250 each, they being indemnified out of the funds of this Company against any loss they may incur thereby.

10th May, 1888
Minute No 16. In reference to Minute No. 10 of the Meeting of the Board held on the 21st March last, it was reported that all necessary steps had been taken to place the control of the Undertaking of the Kingsbridge and Salcombe Railway Company in the new Board constituted of nominees of this Company. After consideration, however, it was thought desirable not to proceed with construction of the Kingsbridge Line until powers have been obtained for the acquisition of the Undertaking by this Company.

A discussion took place as to the Engineer to be employed in the carrying out of the works, and a letter from Mr Wm Lidstone was read stating that he had been connected with the scheme from the first and offering his services, on terms specified, in making surveys and in preparing specifications and working drawings.

The position of Mr Wm Clarke as Engineer of the Kingsbridge and Salcombe Company was referred to, as also the fact of his having been engaged in the purchase of the lands required for the Kingsbridge line - somewhat of an embarrassing situation.

Before taking any steps in the matter the Board desired to obtain information from Mr Clarke with regard to his relations with the Kingsbridge company and as to the progress made with the land purchases, and the Engineering Committee were requested to see Mr Clarke on the subject at their next meeting - diplomatically.

The grand finale of the old company really took place on 21st March, 1888 at a meeting held in the offices of the Great Western Railway at Paddington. The following persons were present at this meeting:

>Mr R. Ilbert in the Chair
>Lt Col. Walker
>Mr E. Fox
>Sir Daniel Gooch Bt
>Sir Alexander Hood
>Mr R. Michell
>Mr A. Hubbard

In Attendance   Mr Nelson   Solicitor Great Western Railway
                  Mr Bayliffe   Solicitor Kingsbridge & Salcombe Railway

It was moved by Mr Fox, seconded by Mr Ilbert and Resolved that Sir Daniel Gooch be and he is hereby elected a Director of the Company in the place of the Earl of Devon. Mr Fox having tendered his resignation, it was Resolved that Sir Alexander Hood be and he is hereby elected a Director of the Company in his stead.

Colonel Walker having tendered his resignation, it was Resolved that Mr Michell be and he is hereby elected a Director of the Company in his stead.

Mr Ilbert having tendered his resignation, it was Resolved that Mr Hubbard be and he is hereby elected a Director of the Company in his stead.

Hereupon the Chair was taken by Sir Daniel Gooch.

It was proposed by Sir Daniel Gooch, seconded by Sir Alexander Hood and Resolved that Mr Ilbert be and he is hereby elected a Director of the Company.

The Minute Book and the Seal of the company were handed to Mr Nelson, the Solicitor of the Great Western Railway.

With all these discussions and meetings of the respective parties taking place the outcome was that the GWR submitted a Bill to Parliament called the 'New Lines Act of 13th August, 1888'. In this Bill powers would be transferred to the Great Western Railway from the Kingsbridge and Salcombe Railway and on 30th May, 1888 the Kingsbridge and Salcombe Board met and decided as follows:

Having regard to the provisions affecting this Company contained in the Great Western Company's Bill now before Parliament,
It was resolved that a special General Meeting of he Shareholders be held at this Station on Wednesday the 13th proximo at 11 o'clock am for the purpose of approving such a Bill and that the necessary notice to that effect be given.

At a special General Meeting held on 13th June, 1888 with Sir Daniel Gooch, Bart in the Chair, the final nail was put in the Kingsbridge and Salcombe Railway's coffin:

The notice convening the meeting having been read and the following Bill having been submitted:
It was resolved that the Bill now submitted to the meeting entitled 'An Act for conferring further powers upon the Great Western Railway Company in connection with their own and other undertakings and upon them and other Companies in connection with undertakings in which they are jointly interested, for vesting in the Great Western Railway Company in undertakings of the Leominster and Bromyard and the Worcester, Bromyard and Leominster Railway Companies, for authorising and confirming agreements with the Kingsbridge and Salcombe and other Railway Companies and for other purposes', be and the same is hereby approved subject to such alterations therein as may be sanctioned by Parliament.

Even before this final meeting of the Kingsbridge and Salcombe Railway the Great Western began the task of arranging and organising all the necessary skills to build the railway. At a Board meeting on 31st May, 1888 a letter was read from Mr Wm Clarke stating:

. . . that he is prepared to make surveys and working drawings, prepare the specification and take all steps necessary in the letting of the Contract and to superintend the construction of the Kingsbridge Line for the sum of £275 per mile, such amount to include his services past and future in the purchase of the lands required for the line.

After discussion the Board agreed to the engagement of Mr Clarke in the carrying out of this work and the Chairman was authorised to conclude an arrangement with him at a remuneration not exceeding £275 per mile to include all services.

Confirmation of Mr Clarke's services and remuneration were confirmed by the Board on 21st June. The payment of £275 per mile was to include the setting out of the line and superintending the construction of the same and of its maintenance for one year after its opening for public traffic. Further to cover all expenses in relation to surveys and the preparation of all contract and other plans, the cost of staff and all charges and expenses of every kind - also all services in connection with land purchases, both past and future.

On completion of the line the Contract Plans, Drawings etc., were to be handed over to the company without extra charge.

The Board of the Great Western Railway finally authorised the completion of the purchase of the land required to build the railway on 25th October. From now on the various committees of the company became involved with all the multitude of problems and the Board maintained only a passing interest in the construction of the railway.

The contractor appointed was Messrs R.T. Rolfe & Son of Plymouth and the estimated total cost was £180,000 - within the budgeted figure of ten years earlier. Work commenced at several points in 1891 as the GWR, having appointed Mr W. Clarke as Engineer, hoped to construct the railway speedily. However, there was no great haste on the part of the contractors.

It is reported that the first sod was cut in January 1891 by Mrs W.P. Arscott of the Royal Oak Hotel, South Brent, at a place known as 'The House in the Way', an old building on Palstone Farm, approximately one mile east of Brent station. It is also said that large quantities of liquor were drunk.

The main works on the line were the cuttings leaving Brent, the embankment each side of Sorley tunnel, the Kingsbridge station area and the numerous bridges mainly over the River Avon.

During the construction of Sorley tunnel considerable problems were encountered by Mr Clarke. There were several fresh water springs in the hillside and on several occasions the works were inundated. The hard stone was withdrawn from both sides and used in building, principally the approach embankments.

There is an interesting story related by Mr John H. Huxham whose family owned Sorley Farm (extracted from the *Western Morning News*):

> During the tunnelling the water supply for the farmhouse, which was by pump, suddenly failed overnight, and on looking around next morning a large hole about 10 ft wide and deep was found only a few yards from the house. Owing to water, the roof of the tunnel had collapsed. A gravitation supply was then laid on from a spring several hundred yards to the north.
>
> My father used to tell us how the orchard at the west end was cut down as part of the first scheme, which failed about 1867, and after a time it was planted again and was fully developed when the 1891 work started, so it was again cut down.

With the building of the line came the navvies and their main base was set up near the Sorley tunnel site and wives and girlfriends, together with their children, arrived also to take up residence. Quarrels were many in this tight knit community, but camp battles were few. There is on record a fight between two wives over a dog. So fierce became their quarrel that the police were called and the wives soon appeared before the court (7th October, 1891) and were bound over to keep the peace.

There was the usual drunkenness, brawls and fights, but no great crimes appear to have been committed, at least not by today's standards. Poaching was the chief pastime of the navvies, there being excellent fishing and game in the luxuriant Avon Valley. Thomas Waling was caught near Loddiswell using explosives to stun the fish. The detonators were stolen from the site and when Mr Waling appeared in court he was charged with stealing explosives and poaching. Being found guilty, he was sentenced to two months for stealing the detonators and three months for poaching, but both sentences were reduced to two months hard labour. Despite the poor transport facilities of the day poor Thomas was put on the 1.15 pm coach to Kingsbridge Road, and began his prison sentence in Exeter Jail that night. Another swift sentence was carried out on John Smith. Found guilty of stealing a pair of boots, value five shillings, he received a sentence of 14 days hard labour. One or two other cases are worth mentioning briefly:

(1) Navvy found in chicken run, claimed only sleeping - fined ten shillings
(2) Navvy caught taking two ducks, 4th October, 1892 - fined
(3) Richard Johns caught with sheep on back, claimed he had just extracted the animal from brambles - fined.

Drunkenness was the cause of most of the clashes by navvies with the law; the results of which were usually fines or short prison sentences. It is pertinent to remember that the local white ale was not only very popular but also very potent.

During 1892 there was an outbreak of smallpox among the navvies. It seems that two navvies moved from Pontypridd to the huts at Gara Bridge to work on the line. As there were between four and five men to a hut, smallpox could soon spread. The isolation of the sufferers contained the outbreak - two going to Braunstone, one to the fever ship at Plymouth, and seven to Modbury.

Accidents were not unknown and six navvies lost their lives during construction. Possibly the most serious accident occurred at Avonwick in August 1891. Whilst blasting out the cutting John Fairchild was buried alive under tons of soil, when the rescuers eventually dug him out he was found to be dead. The funeral took place in Brent on 23rd August, 1891 and 150 workers attended to pay their last respects.

During the severe winter of 1891 the navvies worked hard to clear the snow, especially in Kingsbridge where drifts were up to twelve feet deep. However, one character, known as Rheumatic Skan, was found dead in a barn and at first it was thought through drink, but later he was found to have died of exposure. The snows at Brent were so deep that the 'Zulu' (3.0 pm from Paddington) was snowed up from Monday 9th March until it eventually arrived in Plymouth mid-day on Friday 13th March.

There appeared in the *Western Morning News* of 14th March, 1891 a report of the experiences of the stranded passengers. The spokesman was a traveller who was a representative of a Lancashire company and was angry at the treatment meted out to the passengers:

On Monday night we came along all right, although a little late, until passing Totnes. When we got to Rattray signal box (*sic*) we were delayed for two hours and three-quarters, owing to the block system being out of order. The snow was then falling heavily and the wind extremely strong. We waited all that time for the order to go on to Brent. Our driver finally decided to detach the engine and prospect towards Brent, and having done so, and cleared away some drifts, we were taken there something after eleven o'clock. There were between 30 and 40 passengers and most of us 'put up' in the station all night, lying about in the waiting room, and the rest remaining in the train, which could go no further. We all got there in a very exhausted condition, and were without any refreshments, but the station master went to bed at his usual time, not even asking us to have a cup of tea or coffee, and there is no refreshment room at Brent. Next day a descent was made upon Brent for refreshments, and the inhabitants at once put up everything to famine prices. One gentleman bought a bottle of brandy, for which he

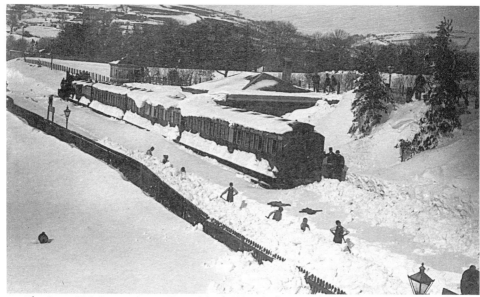

The down 'Zulu' snowed up at Brent, March 1891. At this time the main line was single, with a passing loop at Brent; the train is actually on the up platform line. The primitive conditions for the stranded travellers in such a small station building can well be imagined. There was also a building on the down platform, but it is just out of sight (*to the left*). The signal box, passing loop and refuge sidings were installed in 1875/6.   *C.R. Potts Collection*

A contractor's locomotive near Kingsbridge in the Summer of 1892. Re-railing of the engine would appear to be taking place on a section of temporary track.   *Cookworthy Museum*

had to pay six shillings, the inns charged us double prices for ordinary meats, and some establishments refused to supply us at all, probably thinking that a famine was impending. We returned to the station as best we could, through the great drifts of snow, and with such provisions as we could buy did the best we could, cooking such things as bloaters in the station waiting-room. Our scanty supply, I must say, was most generously supplemented from the small stores which the railway officials, such as the signalmen and others, had with them. There were a number of sailors and soldiers amongst the passengers and most of them were without means. One gentleman gave them a sovereign, and ladies from Brent also brought them money, tobacco, and provisions during our stay. On the following monotonous days we spent our time in smoking and in conversation, and also in 'chaffing' the station master whom we christened 'Dr Parr'. On Wednesday an enterprising amateur photographer from Brent took several views of our snowed up train, with the eighteen or twenty passengers who stuck by it in various prominent positions upon it. We all united in praising the minor officials and the men in charge of the train, for remaining faithful to us, and excused the want of sympathy of 'Dr Parr' on account of his age. The driver kept the fires of his engine going all the time, but his boilers had to be filled with water by hand, and in this work valuable assistance was readily given by the soldiers and marines in the train.

Today, just before we were enabled to leave Brent, we were visited for the first time by the clergyman of the parish, and our final leave taking was celebrated by three sarcastic cheers for 'Dr Parr' and for 'Brent'.

The passengers in this train included Lieutenant Rice, of the Essex Regiment; Mr R. Bayly JP, of Plymouth (who succeeded in getting through to his home on Wednesday), Miss Sykes, and a nurse who was travelling from Scarborough to the South Devon and East Cornwall Hospital, Plymouth.

To continue our story of the building of the line, the Minutes of a meeting of the Locomotive, Carriage and Stores Committee held on 21st December, 1892 contained the following recommendation:

No. 9. That a Contract be made with Messrs K. and K. Bayly for the supply of about 17,000 creosoted sleepers required for the Kingsbridge Railway at the following prices:
On trucks at Plymouth   3s. 0d. each
Delivered at Kingsbridge   3s. 1¼d. each

The Minutes of the Traffic Committee advised that the following expenditure be approved:

No. 22. Construction of Stations and other works connected therewith on the Kingsbridge Railway as follows:

Kingsbridge	£2,720
Avonwick	£855
Gara Bridge	£955
Loddiswell	£880

A tender was submitted from Mr R.J. Rolfe amounting to £5,410 for the construction of the stations and works before mentioned on the Kingsbridge line and under circumstances represented and upon the recommendation of Mr Wm Clarke, authority was given to accept the same.

On 27th April the Traffic Committee gave approval for provision of cast

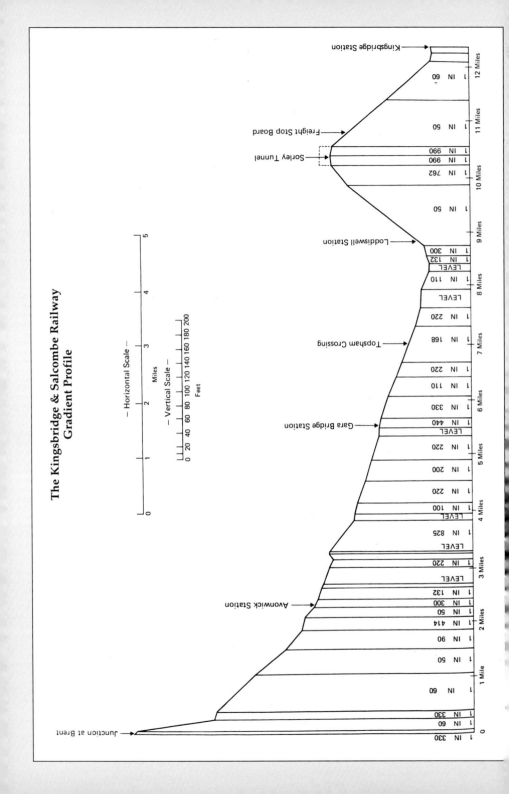

The Kingsbridge & Salcombe Railway
Gradient Profile

weighbridges and cranes for the stations on the Kingsbridge line at a cost of £1,016. Again on 18th May, 1893 they approved the provision of the locking of, and the introduction of the Electric Train Staff on, the Kingsbridge line at an estimated cost of £3314 5s. 0d. Finally on 30th November, 1893, the Minutes of the Traffic Committee contained the following recommendation:

> No. 8. That, as soon as the sanction of the Board of Trade has been obtained, the Kingsbridge Line be opened to Passenger traffic; and the Common Seal of the Company be fixed to an undertaking to the Board of Trade as to the mode of working the Line.

And so we come to the winter of 1893 with the line almost complete. Messrs Rolfe and Son had not been the quickest of builders but the line was ready for inspection by the GWR. Accordingly, on 1st November, a special train was arranged and duly arrived at Brent. We are not told either the type or class of engine and coach, or even the time of departure from Brent, other than mid-morning. It was possibly of SDR origin but we do know there was a proper inspection platform built on the buffer beam of the engine.

The party was as follows:

Mr Wm Clarke	Engineer for GWR supervising building
Mr J. Norris	Assistant Superintendent of the Line
Mr Blackall	Signal Engineer
Mr O. Jones	District Goods Manager
Mr H. Quigley	Traffic Manager
Mr Lloyd	Engineering Department

Together with representatives of R.T. Rolfe and Son

After the inspection of the line, the train returned to Brent at 4.0 pm and all was found to be in order. The final touches were put to the line ready for the official opening on 19th December, 1893.

Before passing on to the opening of the line (in Chapter Three) we must jump ahead a few years for yet another proposal to bring a railway to Kingsbridge. This was an ambitious scheme, well thought out, but which would have been very costly to construct.

In 1895 the plans were laid before Parliament for an enormous network of lines to encompass the South Hams. This scheme involved Totnes Quay, Dartmouth, Salcombe, Kingsbridge and Yealmpton. The Act called 'The Devon South Hams Light Railway Act 1900' was for an extension of Totnes Quay line through Dittisham to Dartmouth (Townstall) where the Dart would be bridged to connect with the Kingswear branch of the GWR, 250 yards north of mile post 227. This bridge was to be of three spans, each 250 feet wide, giving a clearance of 70 feet at high water. Passing through Stoke Fleming, Blackpool Sands, Slapton it would enter Kingsbridge, alongside the GWR station. Here was to be a branch to Salcombe terminating near Salcombe Gas Works, whilst the line itself would carry on to join up with the Yealmpton branch. The line was to be single with passing loops and the gauge was to be 4 ft 8½ in. It was expected that all rolling stock would be provided by the GWR.

The estimated costs of all this development were as follows:

	Miles	Furlongs	Chains	£	s.	d.
Railway one, Kingswear Jn-Kingsbridge	15	1	4.6	198,536	5	0
Railway two Kingsbridge-Yealmpton	12	6	2.3	95,251	10	0
Railway three, Totnes-Dartmouth	6	2	9.3	58,593	10	0
Railway four, Kingsbridge-Salcombe	3	1	9.5	18,749	6	0
				371,130	11	0

An ambitious project fraught with all sorts of problems not least the raising of the necessary funds, and after a short time the proposals were dropped. However, the GWR did consider building the extension to Salcombe from Kingsbridge in the 1920s but the motor bus had proved satisfactory, traffic was developing nicely, and no further proposals were made.

Regrettably Salcombe was never reached by the railway, probably due to the major works required. The proposed route followed the west bank of the Kingsbridge estuary, necessitating a major viaduct from Gerston Point to Heath Point across Collapit Lake and Blanks Lake, in addition to fairly substantial cuttings and embankments, although excavation had started on the station site at Salcombe.

A further proposal for the scheme was to construct a light railway of 2 ft 6 in. gauge some seven miles long, from Kingsbridge station of the GWR, through Charleton, Frogmore, Chillington, Stokenham and Torcross to Slapton Sands ending at the Royal Sands Hotel.

Neither of these schemes became reality, but it would be interesting to muse had the proposal become fact. Kingsbridge could well have become an important junction - should the branch from Yealmpton via Modbury to Kingsbridge have been completed, as it was the Devon South Hams Light Railway's original intention.

Would the narrow gauge extension to the Royal Sands Hotel at Slapton have provided that very necessary extra potential to the 'new' branch? Could it have given life blood to the rather remote Royal Sands Hotel in order that it may have survived today? Unfortunately the Royal Sands Hotel declined rapidly in the 1930s and in fact was virtually destroyed during the allied occupation and manoeuvres of the South Hams in the 1943/4 training scheme. Would Salcombe have benefited by the facilities of the railway? One can only speculate.

Brent station in the late 1890s looking towards Plymouth with the 6-wheeled Kingsbridge branch stock on the left face of the island platform. *Cookworthy Museum*

Chapter Three

The Opening

The line had been completed at an estimated cost of £180,000 and involved some 48 bridges. The official opening took place on 19th December, 1893, and most people were determined to enjoy the event. We do not know of the weather conditions on the great day.

The GWR had allocated 1,000 free tickets to Kingsbridge but no children were allowed to ride on the trains. It therefore meant that at least one member per household could enjoy a ride to Brent and back.

The first train of the day was from Brent, leaving at 8.45 am and the station, signal box and village were gaily decorated with evergreen, flags and bunting. On this first train was Mr C.E. Compton, the Plymouth Traffic Manager and he was given a noisy send off.

At Avonwick, a small crowd from Diptford and Avonwick greeted the arrival of the train and a similar reception was again accorded at Gara Bridge, Loddiswell and Kingsbridge. The crowd of would-be travellers soon took up the empty seats and the train was off back to Brent, running over fog signal detonators at Brent.

At Brent, the official party were waiting to mark the opening and left in the same stock used on the first train of the day. The party was headed by:

Viscount Emlyn	GWR Director
Col C.E. Edgcumbe	GWR Director
Mr Hubbard	GWR Director
H. Lambert	General Manager
C. Inglis	Chief Engineer
C.E. Compton	District Traffic Manager
Mr Quigley	Assistant Traffic Manager
Mr Luxmore	District Loco. Superintendent
Messrs Avery & Jones	Goods Department

Again the train was given a rousing send off. At Loddiswell, the vicar met the party, whilst the vicar of Woodleigh - Revd F.A. Sanders - gave an address of welcome to which Viscount Emlyn replied.

The British School (present Primary School) in Loddiswell, marked the day by having a holiday and in the afternoon a free tea was given to all the children of the Parish. Mr Tapp of the Church School called it a memorable day for the village. In fact in July 1894 the school outing to Brent used the railway for their excursion. One can only hope the weather was fine and dry with the station so far from the village.

On arrival at Kingsbridge the train was met by local dignitaries, headed by the chairman of the Local Board, accompanied by F.B. Mildmay MP, B.W. Sparrow, the Kingsbridge Portreeve, W. Kelland, Dodbroke Portreeve with Messrs J. Veale and N. Pearse, the Town Criers. A guard of honour was provided by the Corps of Rifle Volunteers under Major J. Harris Square. After

The arrival of the double-headed inaugural train, having just passed Kingsbridge's outer home signal, 19th December, 1893.   *Cookworthy Museum*

Officials at Kingsbridge station during opening celebrations including the Town Criers of Kingsbridge and Salcombe resplendent in tricorn hats.   *Cookworthy Museum*

Opening day celebrations on the Quay at Kingsbridge.   *Cookworthy Museum*

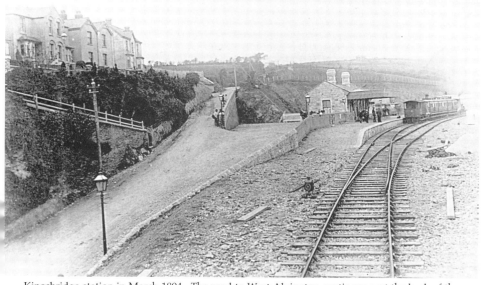

Kingsbridge station in March 1894. The road to West Alvington continues past the back of the station. Note the running line past the end of the station which would have formed part of the abortive extension to Salcombe. *Cookworthy Museum*

A view looking east towards Kingsbridge in the Summer of 1895. Cattle wagons can be seen at the entrance to the goods yard. *Cookworthy Museum*

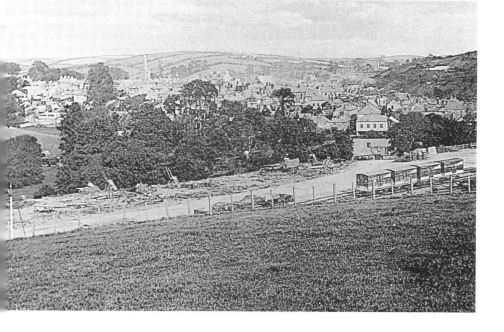

GREAT WESTERN RAILWAY.

On Tuesday, December 19th, 1893, the Branch
Railway from the Brent Station on the South Devon
Section to the town of Kingsbridge, will be opened
for Passenger, Parcels, and Merchandise traffic, and
the following will be the Train Service :—

To Kingsbridge—Week days only.

		a.m.	a m	a m	a m	pm
PADDINGTON	dep.			9 0	11 45	1 15
Bristol	,,	6 15	7 0	12 5	2 30	4 3
Exeter	,,	8 40	10 31	1 50	4 12	5 45
Torquay	,,	9 22	11 30	2 57	4 30	6 32
Newton Abbott	,,	9 42	12 5	3 20	5 10	6 50
Brent	arr.	10 18	12 42	3 56	5 47	7 27
PLYMOUTH	dep.	9 10	12 5	2 35	4 15	7 15
Brent	arr.	9 57	12 54	3 17	5 4	8 3
Brent	dep.	10 25	1 2	4 5	5 55	8 11
Avonwick	,,	10 37	1 10	4 13	6 3	8 21
Gara Bridge	,,	10 50	1 19	4 22	6 12	8 37
Loddiswell	,,	11 6	1 30	4 33	6 23	8 42
KINGSBRIDGE	arr.	11 18	1 42	4 45	6 35	8 59

From Kingsbridge—Week days only.

KINGSBRIDGE	dep.	8 0	11 40	2 32	4 55	6 42
Loddiswell	,,	8 16	11 51	2 43	5 8	6 53
Gara Bridge	,,	8 31	12 2	2 54	5 21	7 4
Avonwick	,,	8 45	12 12	3 4	5 34	7 14
Brent	arr.	8 53	12 20	3 12	5 42	7 22
Brent	dep	8 59	12 44	3 58	5 49	7 29
PLYMOUTH	arr	9 46	1 30	4 40	6 33	8 13
Brent	dep	9 19	12 28	3 18		8 6
Newton Abbot	arr	9 47	12 52	3 50		8 38
Torquay	,,	10 9	1 28	4 12		9 2
Exeter	,,	11 30	1 41	4 47		9 38
Bristol	,,	12 10	3 38	6 45		12 35
PADDINGTON	,,	2 53	6 30	10 3		4 0

Timetable of the opening of the line 1893.

Timetable for the first quarter of 1902.

KINGSBRIDGE BRANCH.

Down Trains.		Week Days only.						Up Trains		Week Days only.					
		a.m.	a.m.		p.m.		p.m.	p.m.	p.m.			a.m.	a.m.	a.m.	p.m.	p.m.	p.m.	
Brent	dep	9 20	10 30		1 10		4 5	6 15	8 18	Kingsbridge (for Salcombe)	dep	8 0	9 15	11 60	2 30	5 5	7 15
Avonwick	,,	9 27	10 37	Mixed	1 18	Mixed	4 12	6 22	8 25	Loddiswell	,,	8 11	9 26	11 51	2 41	5 17	7 26
Gara Bridge	,,	9 35	10 45		1 27		4 20	6 30	8 32	Gara Bridge	,,	8 19	9 35	11 59	2 69	5 27	7 36
Loddiswell	,,	9 43	10 55		1 37		4 36	6 35	8 41	Avonwick	,,	8 27	9 43	12 7	2 57	5 35	7 52
Kingsbridge (for Salcombe)	arr	9 55	11 7		1 50		4 40	6 50	8 53	Brent	arr	8 35	9 51	12 15	3 5	6 56	7 50

a speech of welcome by Mr J.S. Hurrell, the official party climbed into horse-drawn coaches and the procession, headed by the Regimental Band of the King's Own Scottish Borderers (KOSB), proceeded round the gaily decorated streets.

Eventually the party arrived at the Town Hall for lunch, which was provided by Mr H.W. Thomas of the King's Arms Hotel. We do not know the menu for the lunch, but there were numerous speeches and toasts. Mr W. Clarke - the Engineer of the line - was congratulated on his skill, not only as an Engineer, but as a skilful land negotiator and in handling the many problems during the building, not least the water in Sorley tunnel.

During the afternoon, the KOSB Band played in the bandstand on the quay, whilst the town band marched round the town playing lively airs. At 9 o'clock the church bells of St Edmund Kingsbridge, St Thomas of Dodbrooke and All Saints, West Alvington, simultaneously rang out a peal of welcome.

A rugby football match was played between Kingsbridge and Totnes in the afternoon at the club field (W. Alvington Hill) with over 600 spectators - admission charge 2d. The home side won by one goal and one try to one penalty goal and one try.

In the evening a mile long procession formed up at Manor House - leaving at 6.0 pm - proceeding through Kingsbridge and Dodbrooke, ending at the Quay. This was followed by a firework display staged at Tacket Wood. The fortunate townsfolk having tickets then went to an invitation dance at the King's Arms.

The Volunteers had their own celebration. Gathering at the armoury at 8.0 pm they had a cold supper provided by Major Harris Square, which was followed by dancing.

And so the day ended and Kingsbridge had its railway.

The railway was soon in business, being well used by the townsfolk. So much so that on one day over Christmas, 300 passengers booked tickets and as many people came into Kingsbridge. The outcome of this rush was that on 27th December, 20 workmen moved in to widen the carriageway, cutting back the bank against the Salcombe Road, and the building of a retaining wall. In 1894 the Great Western improved the station by providing extra siding accommodation and separate cattle facilities at a cost of £5,000.

An unidentified 'Duke' class 4-4-0 hauling an express from Plymouth approaching Brent around the turn of the century.   *L&GRP*

A Foals & Tucker's coach awaits business from a down train *c*. 1895.   *Cookworthy Museum*

Traps and carriages awaiting London passengers and goods in the Summer of 1898. Note the original station buildings.   *Cookworthy Museum*

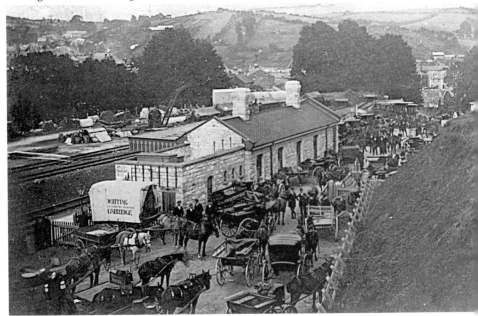

On 25th February, 1894, a serious landslide occurred at Avonwick. Some 2,000 yards of bank slipped onto the line just after the 10.25 am from Kingsbridge had passed. Mr Loosemore, the station master at Avonwick, acted promptly, cancelling the 11.40 am up and 1.2 pm down trains and by getting workmen for repairs. So swiftly did he act and the work was so speedily completed, that the 2.32 up and the 4.5 pm down were able to run.

Publicity, always a strong point of the GWR, was soon being used to promote trips, cheap tickets etc. For example:

12th May - cheap trip to London on 11.50 train, returning on 19th May.
23rd/24th/25th May - Trips to Devon County Show at Exeter.
24th May - Cheap trip to Plymouth, celebrating the Queen's birthday.

However, all was not well with the running of trains and in August, complaints were being made of branch trains arriving after or departing before connections with the main line. The GWR soon resolved these problems and the branch continued to prosper.

The *Kingsbridge Gazette* reported on 7th February, 1896, from the Minutes of the Council meeting, the Chairman Mr J.S. Hurrell as saying that when the railway opened the GWR had 'promised to do a great deal' for Kingsbridge, especially with regard to its agricultural interests. Mr Hurrell did not agree that this had been the case and instructed the Council to take the matter up with the railway company. Remarks were also made about the 40 minutes wait passengers from Paddington experienced at Newton Abbot awaiting the Brent and Kingsbridge train:

Newton was a nasty disagreeable draughty station, in fact the 3.00 from Paddington passed through Brent just as the Kingsbridge train was about to leave - could it not be stopped.

The rather cramped cattle dock facilities were also a major bone of contention, the GWR agreeing to improve matters within 'two months'.

There was a constant complaint of the lack of refreshment facilities at Brent - echoed many times over the next sixty years.

A Poem to Commemorate the Opening of the Railway

The Kingsbridge Railway

Old Kingsbridge is in fete to day,
If you listen awhile you'll hear folks say,
The GWR has been so kind,
They've been an opened our new line,
For Christmas don't you see is nigh,
The managers winked the other eye,
For true as I'm a living sinner
We're drawing near to Christmas dinner.

A down train near Avonwick being hauled by a 'Metro' class 2-4-0T.

Dermot Reynolds Collection

Avonwick station with a 'Metro' about to leave with a down train *c.* 1900.   *Lens of Sutton*

CHORUS
There was Dodbrooke Dolly, and Kingsbridge Kate,
They got to the station just too late,
But Woodleigh Weenie, and Loddiswell Liz,
With Topsham Lilly, all in a friz,
They got to the station just in time
And had their ride right up the line.

But come wee'l hurry to the station,
To see what's all the consternation
A ticket Sir; free, thanks, with pleasure,
The GWR's, a proper treasure,
We take our seats, bang! bang! the doors,
The whistle sounds, the engine roars,
And from the throats of the gather'd crowd,
Goes up a cheer both long and loud.

Chorus - There was Dodbrooke Dolly, &c.

Kingsbridge is quickly left behind,
And 'Sorley Tunnel', soon wee'l find,
Lor now my dears don't kick up a fuss,
For christen this 'Tunnel' you know we muss
The officials have acted very kind
And all the lights are left behind,
So into the 'Tunnel' we go with a drash
And out we come with a regular crash.

Chorus - There was Dodbrooke Dolly, &c.

Red faces, hats, and bonnets away,
What Sir, did you ask the reason why?
Was ever such Rip van Winkle, under the sun?
Don't you know the lasses, love the fun,
Besides we're all on pleasure bent,
And did'nt expect, that you'd be sent,
To spoil our fun and frolic to day,
Pass on if you please, get out of the way.

Chorus - There was Dodbrooke Dolly, &c.

Now on past Loddiswell and Topsham quick
To Gara Bridge and Avonwick,
In Brent we quickly are set down,
To wander o'er and o'er the town,
To think of 'Joe' and his coach and four,
That will travel to station, never more,
A good job too, do I hear some say,
But coaches are all very well in a way.

Chorus - There was Dodbrooke Dolly, &c.

An unidentified 2-6-2T awaits departure from Kingsbridge *c.* 1900.   *Cookworthy Museum*

2-6-2T No. 3101 glistens in the sun at Kingsbridge. At this time, *c.* 1905, the carriage shed has still to be built. The locomotive was built in 1905, later being renumbered 4401.

Ken Nunn/LCGB Collection

Till its time to go back by train to town,
We join in the chorus all the way down
Of After the Ball, and Daisy Bell,
You say pleased with yer ride, yes very well,
But Dodbrooke Dolly and Kingsbridge Kate
Was heard to say, that night quite late,
That they'd take a ride right up one day,
When all the common folk was away.

Chorus - There was Dodbrooke Dolly, &c.

Twenty years and more have wainted we
This opening festival to see,
But surely better late than never,
And nought us two shall ever sever,
Lock up the workshop, close the store,
Tie up the horses, bolt the door,
Come old and young, come grave and gay,
Let this be a real, *Red Letter Day*.

CHORUS - FINAL

Then Dodbrooke Dolly and Kingsbridge Kate,
Will tell their children soon or late,
How the line was opened in ninety three,
And Weenie, and Lizzie, and Tilly, agree,
To gather their children all around,
And tell the same story I'll be bound.

A class '44XX', probably No. 4410, poses with the Brent station master and footplate crew
c. 1910 on the branch face of the island platform.   *Dermot Reynolds Collection*

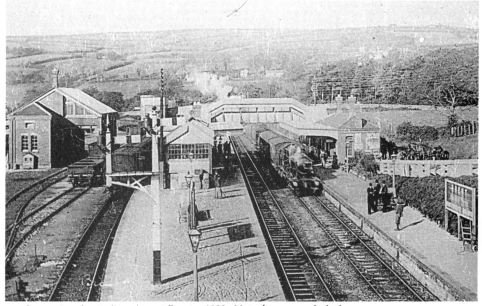

An up stopping train arrives at Brent *c.* 1900. Note the unpaved platforms.

Cookworthy Museum

'Manor' class 4-6-0 No. 7820 *Dinmore Manor* hauls an up express whilst 2-6-2T No. 5532 waits with the 12.34 pm to Kingsbridge on the branch face of the island platform at Brent, 21st May, 1956. *P.W. Gray*

Chapter Four

Speed to the West

Imagine a sunny day in 1936. The scene, platform 1, Paddington station, the time 10.25 am. Our train is in the platform, a pannier tank at the buffer stops. The station master resplendent in top hat and tails, immaculate 'Centenary' coaches in chocolate and cream. The locomotive is 4-6-0 No. 6009 *King Charles II*, the polished brass, copper and steel gleaming in the morning sun. We take our seats in the Exeter portion - the coach roof boards labelled Paddington-Kingsbridge. 10.29, signals off, whistles blow, our guard - complete with red rose in buttonhole - waves his flag, the clock on Platform 1 clicks to 10.30 am, and we are off. On our journey we drop off the Weymouth and Minehead slip portions and soon it is our turn to leave the 'Limited' main train at Exeter.

At Exeter, a 'Hall' class 4-6-0 backs down (perhaps No. 4977 *Watcombe Hall*), couples onto our train with a few more coaches and we are soon on our way along the Exe estuary, passing through Dawlish and Teignmouth into Newton Abbot. Now the exhaust beat changes as we climb Dainton bank and stop at Totnes. Away again climbing up Rattery and into Brent station where our coach is detached. The branch locomotive runs out, couples on, and shunts us onto the 'B' set in the bay, or No. 3 platform, ready for our run down the branch.

Brent station was first opened in 1848, but was not the station for Kingsbridge. In those early days, Wrangaton station was called Kingsbridge Road and the stage coaches met trains there.

Brent has changed over the years. Built by the SDR, the original station building was on the down platform and with the opening of branch in 1893, much alteration took place. The main line was originally single but was doubled in 1893 when the new main station buildings were built on the up platform. It is this rebuilt station we are able to describe more fully in this book.

The entire station was situated between two road overbridges under the shadow of Brent Hill, on the edge of the village, with an access road to the station and goods yard from both bridges. The up platform, starting at the Totnes end contained a water crane which was alongside the starting signal. Then there was an attractive station garden with flowers, palm trees and the traditional GWR platform seat and name board. Up against the end wall of the station building, of red and blue engineering brick with a slated roof, were climbing roses.

The building contained a ladies room, a combined booking hall/main waiting room, a booking office, station master's office and gents' toilet, all under a canopy. Access was via a wicket gate under a roof in between the station building and the covered footbridge. Beyond the bridge were a collection of huts, being for lamp room, cycles and stores; a ramp at the Plymouth end led to the walkway over the up and down lines over which porters wheeled those heavy GWR platform trolleys.

The down or island platform contained, from the Plymouth end, starting signal, water crane, usual platform furniture, and again palm trees whilst the

2-6-2T No. 3104 (later renumbered 4404) shunting at Brent in 1906. Note narrowed broad gauge track.   *R.G. Carpenter Collection*

No. 5573 collects coaches for Kingsbridge from the rear of 11.00 am Paddington-Newquay train, 29th August, 1959.   *T.W. Nicholls*

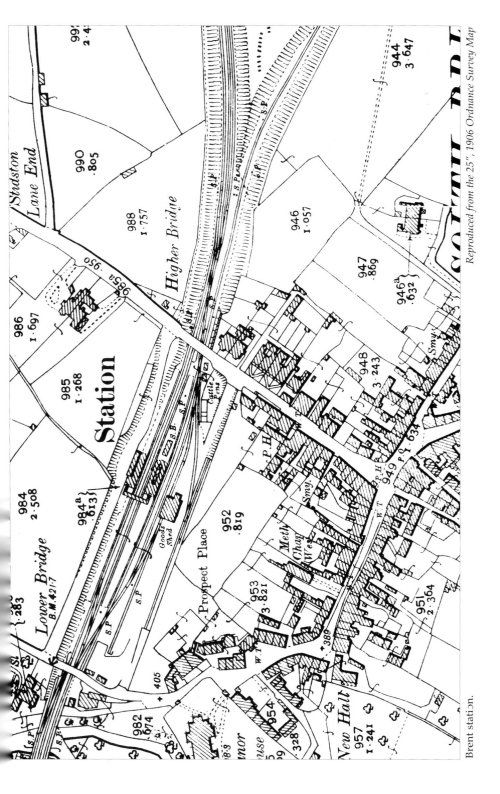

Brent station.

No. 4568 leaves Brent with the 3.15 pm for Kingsbridge, 7th April, 1958. *P.W. Gray*

'County' class 4-6-0 No. 1021 *County of Montgomery* approaches Brent with a down express on 15th July, 1958. The Kingsbridge branch diverges off to the right. *R.C. Riley*

No. 5558 approaching Avonwick with the down 6.10 pm from Brent, 16th August, 1958.

P.W. Gray

No. 4561 approaches Avonwick on the 10.10 am from Brent as it passes under the Plymouth-Totnes road on 27th May, 1961.

P.W. Gray

Avonwick station looking towards Brent *c*. 1915.   *L&GRP*

An up train approaches Avonwick station headed by a '44XX' Class 2-6-2T *c*. 1920.

Lens of Sutton

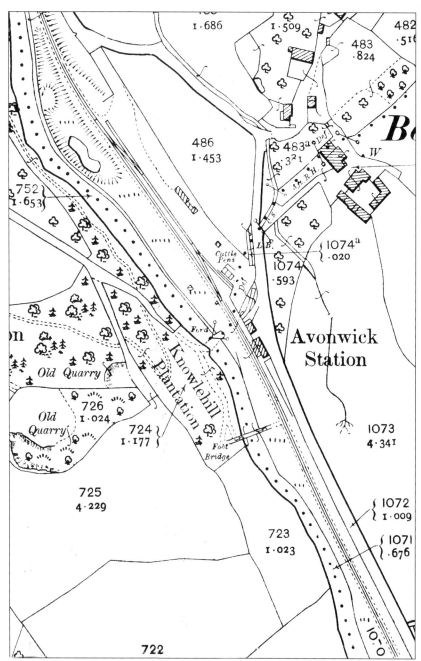

Avonwick station.

Reproduced from the 25', 1906 Ordnance Survey Map

footbridge led into the old broad gauge building which contained the toilets, waiting room and staff room and alongside this was Brent signal box. A large box with brick base and the characteristic Great Western windows containing 66 levers on the operating floor, under which was the locking room.

In the goods.yard at the Totnes end, between the platform and road access were two huts for the signal and telegraph department, the cattle pens and loading gauge whilst the goods shed, again in red and blue brick with slated roof, had an extension housing a two storey office block. Within the shed was a crane for loading and unloading wagons and lorries. At the Plymouth end of the yard were end and side loading facilities also a water tank on the roof of a stores building and alongside was a black timbered building belonging to a local trader.

We now return to our train, the driver of which has already been handed the token Brent-Gara Bridge. The branch makes a trailing connection on the down side of the main line, so we must reverse our direction. Whistles blow and we are off.

Leaving Brent, the main line curves left down hill to Totnes, whilst we have a short straight stretch of line in a cutting and down hill, then curving right we soon dive under the A38 trunk road. We pass through hilly countryside on an embankment but a falling gradient until we pass under the A385 at Avonwick and join the River Avon - our constant companion for the next eight miles or so. However, Avonwick station is really in between Diptford and Avonwick - a sort of no man's land - in reality the area is known as Beneknowle. Stopping at Avonwick, 2 miles, 36 chains from Brent, a look at the station reveals the style of architecture for all stations on the branch. The station building is stone and has a canopy with a single platform face. The building has a booking office, toilet, waiting room and small goods office. However, in the yard we find the first of the three camping coach sites here but no signals. The river is on our right and in spring the banks are full of primroses, violets and bluebells.

Leaving Avonwick, we continue southwards in a succession of reverse curves which carry the line over the river into a wooded valley. The unique rural charm of this branch is now quite apparent to the traveller. From spring to autumn, the hillside, the woodlands, the white painted farm dwellings and the rich green pasture of the Avon valley portray an idyllic setting of this Devonshire branch. Twisting through woodland we cross and re-cross the river until deep between two hillsides, a blast on the engine whistle warns Gara Bridge (5 miles 39 chains from Brent) of our impending arrival. Now on a left-hand curve we pass first the fixed distant and then the home signal to run over a level crossing and into the station. As with all intermediate stations, the main buildings are on the downside.

This station was one of the most picturesque on the old GWR lying in the trough of a wooded valley, the river going under the stone humped-backed road bridge and describing a semi-circle around the line before diving under the track beyond the station and then curving the opposite way. On the upside, alongside the level crossing, is Gara Bridge signal box. This box is identical in appearance to Kingsbridge, but contained 24 levers and controlled the level crossing with its associated wheel and locking devices. The layout was fully

No. 4561 on the 11.00 am to Brent passes Diptford, 1st August, 1960. *P.W. Gray*

No. 4561 with the 2.30 pm from Brent passes Broadley Farm on 5th March, 1960. Note the farmer's occupation crossing. *P.W. Gray*

A pre-World War II view of Gara Bridge station. Note the clerestory roofed camping coach at the south end of the station. *D.J. Hyde Collection*

A view looking west across Gara Bridge station showing the signal box and level crossing at the north end of the station. *Dermot Reynolds Collection*

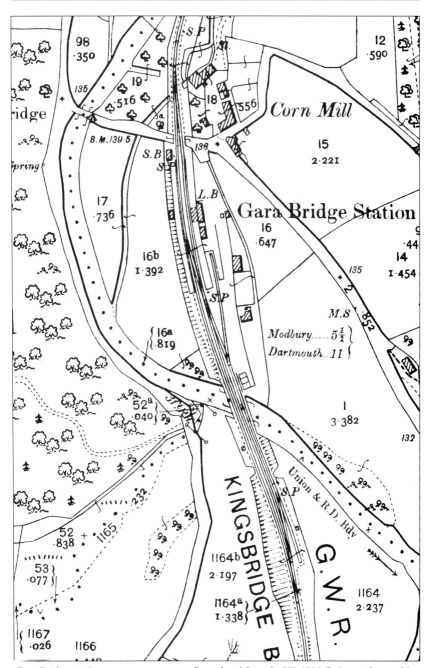

Gara Bridge station.   *Reproduced from the 25', 1906 Ordnance Survey Map*

Gara Bridge signal box and crossing gates, view looking towards Brent *c.* 1950.

BR/OPC Joint Venture

The station building at Gara Bridge *c.* 1960.　　　　　*W. Beard/Dermot Reynolds Collection*

Gara Bridge station looking towards Brent *c*. 1950.   *BR/OPC Joint Venture*

Gara Bridge station looking towards Kingsbridge with camping coaches in the bay platform, one a toplight, the other a clerestory; *c*. 1950.   *OPC*

No. 4561 departs Gara Bridge with the 2.30 pm from Brent on 8th June, 1961. Note the signal has already been returned to danger.	*P.W. Gray*

Looking south towards Loddiswell *c.* 1958 - the retaining wall was built during construction to avoid building two further river overbridges. The original river bed lies to the left of the line.
Dermot Reynolds Collection

signalled, and in its later years tall fir trees grew on the platforms and with its
well kept gardens, the station looked a real picture. In the siding adjoining the
station were stabled one, and frequently two, camping coaches. It was possible
to cross trains of approximately 10 coaches in length at Gara Bridge (this being
the normal crossing point on the branch). There is a lovely passenger shelter on
the up platform of wood and stone construction.

Hazelwood House at Gara Bridge is the home of the Peak family who keenly
supported the railway. Richard Peak (sometime Sheriff of London) sold part of
his lands to the company and later the family used the trains. In the final years
the children from the estate used to be brought to Gara station to take the train
to school in Kingsbridge. However, on the return journey any bad behaviour
was rewarded by the guilty party having to walk home - all uphill.

Off again along the valley over the river, we curve right and are soon passing
through Hazelwood and to the second level crossing at Topsham Bridge
crossing. A very picturesque spot with a granite road bridge over the Avon.
This was a rather remote spot, the railway providing a house for the crossing
keeper on the banks of the river, a pleasant yet lonely place. After crossing the
valley, the hills close in again on the line, affording minimal clearance with the
river bank - a constant problem with erosion of the trackbed kept the permanent
way gang fully occupied - at this point.

The valley then opens out to the west with thick woods to the east. After
crossing the river and negotiating a further series of reverse curves, the river
tumbling down below the line, we run into Loddiswell (pronounced Lodswell).
The station (8 miles 65 chains from Brent) is built on similar lines to Avonwick,
but on the opposite hillside from the village, indeed the goods yard was cut out
of the hillside. The station was on a slight curve and again in the bay nearest
the station, camping coaches were to be found.

The station of Loddiswell was in fact nearer to the Parish of Woodleigh -
Loddiswell being a hard mile's walk away, mostly uphill.

The river now falls away to the west, having been crossed by the railway no
fewer than 10 times, as the line strikes uphill to the watershed between the
Avon and the Kingsbridge estuary.

The bark of the locomotive is now quite evident as she blasts her way up the
1 in 50 gradient on a long curved embankment - crossing the main
Kingsbridge/Brent Road (B3196) to the south-east to gain a hillside location and
affording passengers on the western side the final glimpse of the Avon running
'for the sea' at Aveton Gifford, then a short cutting to burrow into the major
engineering work of the line - Sorley tunnel 625 yards long. Just outside the
tunnel is a freight stop board for pinning wagon brakes down as required, as
the cutting changes to an embankment the train passes the Kingsbridge fixed
distant on a falling gradient of 1 in 50 - the summit being about the centre of the
tunnel. Out on to the embankment, there is a fine prospect across to the sea and
still on a falling gradient the Brent road crosses the line, half a mile of straight
line follows then the line passes under the Plymouth road (A379); an
embankment followed by a short cutting and we pass the outer home signals of
Kingsbridge, turning on an embankment to the south-east into Kingsbridge
station, perched above the town on a hillside beside the Salcombe Road. Our

No. 4561 departs Loddiswell with the 11.00 am from Kingsbridge on 16th April, 1960. The camping coaches are already in place for the forthcoming Summer season. *P.W. Gray*

Loddiswell station looking towards Kingsbridge in May 1961. *Lens of Sutton*

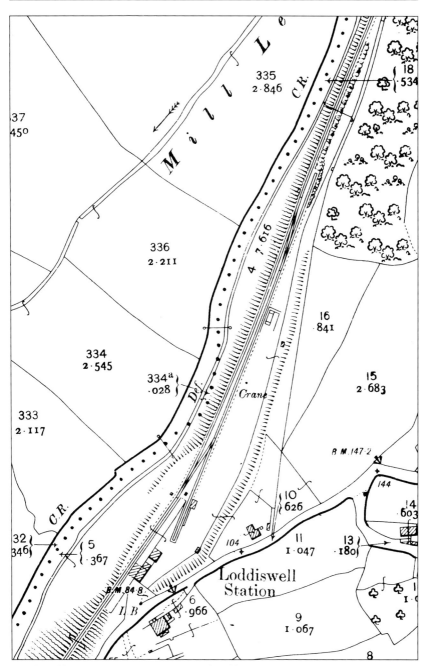

Loddiswell station.   *Reproduced from the 25", 1906 Ordnance Survey Map*

Loddiswell station with station master's house in the background *c.* 1910.
Dermot Reynolds Collection

A '45XX' class 2-6-2T climbs to Sorley tunnel with the 10.10 am from Brent, 3rd June, 1961.
P.W. Gray

Another view of the 10.10 am from Brent, this time a little further up the incline on the approach to Sorley tunnel, 16th April, 1960. *P.W. Gray*

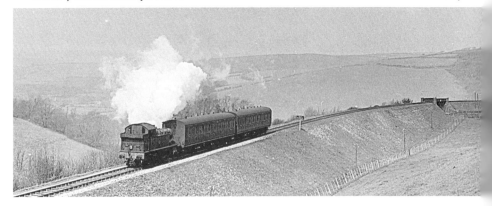

A view of Sorley tunnel mouth from the north. *L&GRP*

'45XX' 2-6-2T No. 5520 with an up working in the cutting prior to Sorley tunnel, August 1961.
R.E. Toop

The throat of the station at Kingsbridge in the 1950s showing the signal box and bay platform starting signal. *OPC*

No. 5558 leaves Kingsbridge with the up 12.35 pm to Brent on 15th July, 1958. *R.C. Riley*

A 1950s view looking north towards the signal box and goods shed at Kingsbridge. *OPC*

2-6-2T No. 5552 leaves Kingsbridge in the Summer of 1957. *BR/OPC Joint Venture*

2-6-2T No. 5505 leaves Kingsbridge with an up train in the Summer of 1957.

D.S. Green/Dermot Reynolds Collection

The 5.10 pm for Brent stands at Kingsbridge in September 1958. *M. Hale*

No. 5525 about to run round its train at Kingsbridge, 26th August, 1961. The carriage shed can be clearly seen to the left. *R.C. Riley*

Kingsbridge station building from the trackbed *c.* 1960. *W. Beard/Dermot Reynolds Collection*

2-6-2T No. 5573 runs round its train at Kingsbridge, 2nd August, 1960.   *R.E. Toop*

A view along the station platform at Kingsbridge.   *W. Beard/Dermot Reynolds Collection*

Kingsbridge carriage shed from the end of the bay platform, *c.* 1960.
W. Beard/Dermot Reynolds Collection

The road motor building after closure. The siding at the rear is where the Saturday through coaches were stored until required. *Ken Williams*

Kingsbridge Station - Original Layout

Taken from Official Plan

Final layout at Kingsbridge (from 1924)

Taken from Official Plan

GRADIENT SECTION

KEY PLAN

Kingsbridge signal box *c*. 1960. Opened in 1893 with 25 levers, a new frame (with 33 levers) was installed in 1915. *W. Beard/Dermot Reynolds Collection*

Kingsbridge goods shed *c*. 1960. *W. Beard/Dermot Reynolds Collection*

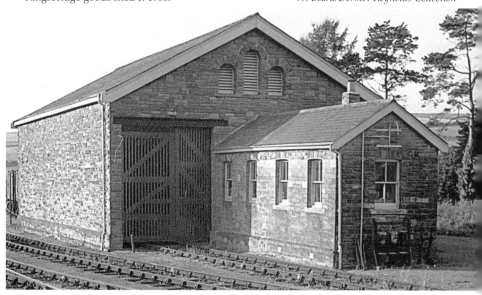

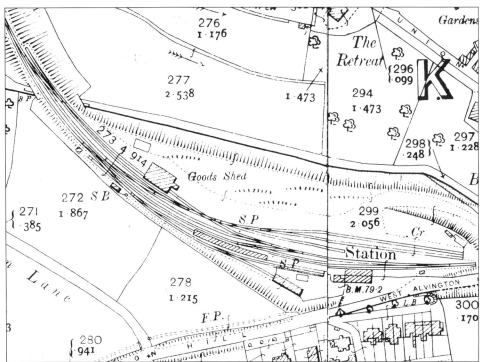

Kingsbridge station.   *Reproduced from the 25", 1906 Ordnance Survey Map*

The collection of huts near Kingsbridge engine shed *c.* 1958.   *Ken Williams*

Kingsbridge station and engine shed from the road *c.* 1958, with the station master's car to the right.
Ken Williams

Kingsbridge station building detail.
W. Beard/Dermot Reynolds Collection

journey's end.

On the Salcombe Road side of the station, the land rises sharply up a grassy bank to fields looking west and north over the town. The view is typically the Devon of gently rolling hills and fields.

The final layout of the station consisted of a curved main platform with an engine release road and a bay platform, off which came a spur to the locomotive shed.

The goods yard has several roads and is equipped with a goods shed, cattle dock, animal feed store, yard crane, and a small carriage shed, together with the usual collection of small huts and old coach bodies on concrete blocks. At the extreme north-eastern end of the yard are a number of racks for the storing of wooden telegraph poles for the GPO.

The station building is constructed of a light grey stone and is in two distinct parts. On the platform side, underneath the canopy, the doors are as follows, starting at the western end of the block; left luggage and parcels office - unmarked - (this part added during the rebuilding of the station), gentlemen, ladies room, booking office, enquiries and advance booking office, station master. A small sliding bar platform scale is fixed flush on the right of the door of the left luggage and parcels office. On the end wall nearest the shed are kept fire buckets, whilst there is also the usual typical platform furniture. The west end of the building was extended in the late 1940s.

The engine shed, which is constructed of a similar material to the station building, will accommodate one 2-6-2T only. It has no windows, but roof lights are provided with five square ventilating shafts mounted on the roof, together with an inspection pit provided inside the shed.

Immediately outside the engine shed is the water tower to supply the water crane at the western end of the platform, a locomotive coaling stage, and an ash pit set between the rails in front of the water tower.

The carriage shed is on the adjacent line to that used for running round, being of black corrugated iron construction without windows, and capable of holding two passenger coaches. The metal sheeting finishes some 2 to 3 ft from the ground, also acting as a waiting room for the Western National bus passengers waiting to travel on the buses to Salcombe and Hope Cove, Dartmouth and Plymouth. Originally this shed was sited near the signal box but was moved when the station layout was altered.

Level with the carriage shed, on the next line, is the animal feed store, occupied by Silcock's, the cattle, pig and poultry food suppliers. The building, made at Exeter, is of pre-cast concrete construction and has its own small unloading platform on the track side, with two large doors on the opposite side. However, this was added only in the early 1950s.

The cattle dock is situated at the north-eastern end of the yard and had a large black corrugated iron shed alongside it. The shed, which served as a fodder and bedding store for cattle to be transported, is open at the eastern end, and is of similar construction to the carriage shed previously mentioned, but differs in that windows are provided in the sides and it is also used for garaging the lorries.

The coal siding occupies part of the rear line behind the cattle dock, but no coal bunkers are provided, and the method of unloading the wagons was by a

2-6-2T No. 5533 on the 2.10 pm for Brent, 21st May, 1956. *P.W. Gray*

No. 4561 on shed at Kingsbridge, 28th August, 1960. *M. Hale*

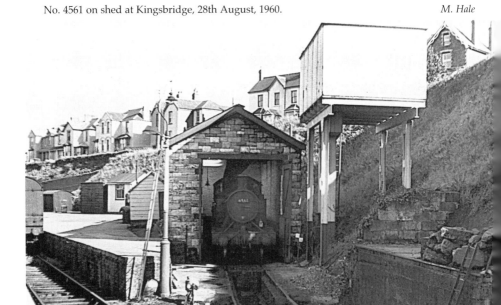

tractor fitted with a mechanical shovel, the latter being thrust into the open side doors of the trucks. The load acquired was then dumped into a waiting coal lorry; the bagging of the coal was presumably done in the coal merchant's own yard away from the station.

A large stone goods shed with spacious offices attached, stands towards the western end of the yard inside which is the usual crane, and an outside siding is provided at the rear of the goods shed.

The lower half of the signal cabin at the south-western end of the station is of stone construction, the upper half being of wood and painted in GWR colours.

The signals are typical of the GWR, and there are several interesting arms in use as well as the usual disc type. However, there is no apparatus for picking up or setting down the token. (Neither is there this facility at Gara Bridge.) The normal practice was for the signalman to leave his box and hand over the token to the locomotive crew.

Avonwick was demoted to a halt after nationalisation - traffic in later years being virtually non-existent and, when the sidings were removed, it lost its camping coaches.

Loddiswell and Gara Bridge kept their camping coaches until the end of the summer of 1961. Loddiswell was demoted to a halt in 1962.

Topsham crossing was protected by distant signals. The signal lamp had a winding mechanism which enabled the reservoir to be replenished, merely by winding down the entire lamp unit.

The gatekeeper's house, although close to the Avon, had no water supply other than by churns brought by the afternoon up goods from Kingsbridge. The local authority in fact made arrangements for a water supply shortly before the branch closed! Officially the branch speed limit was 35 mph.

Kingsbridge engine shed and water tower c. 1960.   *W. Beard/Dermot Reynolds Collection*

Ponies wait to be loaded at Brent *c*. 1910. The branch train in the background is made up mostly of 4-wheeled stock.

Ken Williams Collection

Horses being lead to the Kingsbridge station in 1914.

Dermot Reynolds Collection

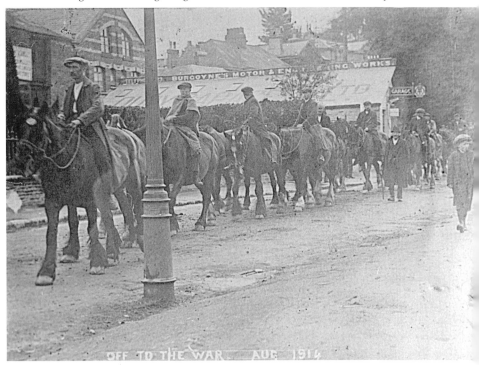

Chapter Five

Branch Traffic and Operations

We have already outlined the operations and the changes which took place after the opening. It is now appropriate to review the working of the branch over the years it was in operation. It is not very easy to establish much concerning the traffic in the early years but an attempt has been made to give as full a picture as possible.

There were the normal weekday passenger services operating making connections at Brent with main line services, and also freight trains. Some of the passenger trains however were marked 'mixed' in the time table - that is to say they could carry goods vehicles on passenger trains. Initially there were no Sunday movements on the branch, but in June 1905 a service operated as follows:

| Brent | *dep.* | 4.20 pm | Kingsbridge | *dep.* | 6.20 pm |
| Kingsbridge | *arr.* | 4.55 | Brent | *arr.* | 6.55 |

This service ran with slight variations until March 1912 when it was withdrawn due to the coal strike. The service was reinstated in May 1913 with a London connection as follows:

| Plymouth | *dep.* | 2.30 pm | Kingsbridge | *dep.* | 5.00 pm |
| Kingsbridge | *arr.* | 4.00 | Plymouth | *arr.* | 6.25 |

Again there were slight variations to the running times over the ensuing years but in 1918 this service was taken off and never ran again.

With the outbreak of the 1914-18 war, troops came to the South Hams for training and brought additional traffic to the branch. As a result of the carnage in France, horses were required to make good the casualties suffered by the transport regiments. A decree was issued and all farmers were required to bring their horses to the quay for inspection. Eventually several hundred horses were selected and were led to the station for dispatch to the army for training. About 1917 a similar happening took place when beef cattle were required to provide food for the army.

Alas, we know little of operations during this early period of the branch history and know only that the normal trade was carried on: e.g. grain, mechanical equipment, livestock, stone, timber and so on being conveyed by the trains. There was a healthy growth in the demand for the facilities of the GWR, and the local staff were keen to encourage new traffic.

During the coal strike of 1912 fuel was extremely scarce, and economies were made. From March, the 7.30 pm to Brent and the 8.45 pm ex-Brent were cancelled giving five services each way daily, with suspension of the Sunday service. In April services were again reduced to four services each way with the cancellation of the 9.15 am to Brent and 10.02 am ex-Brent. However, by 29th

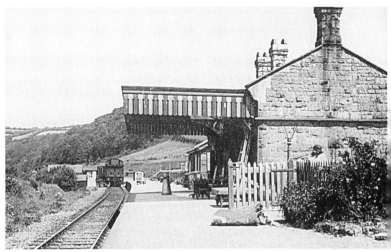

Right: Loddiswell station looking towards Brent with a down train approaching, 10th June, 1921.
Lens of Sutton

Above: Camping Coach visitors with the station master at Gara Bridge *c.* 1962.
Ken Williams Collection

Right: Loddiswell goods yard in the 1950s looking towards Brent with camping coaches in the bay platform.
BR/OPC Joint Venture

April it was possible to resume normal services, except for the Sunday trains.

In the mid-1920s local farmers were encouraged to take their cider apples by train to a local cider brewery at Abbotskerswell. However, Devon is a cider County and only unwanted apples were sent, as most farmers could use up all they grew. But good crops caused a surplus and during the later 1920s as much as 1,000 tons of cider apples were loaded into wagons for Newton Abbot where they were transhipped to Henly's Brewery later to become part of the Whiteways empire. Road transport competition killed this trade in the 1930s.

The traffic in rabbits was quite considerable and a loaded van was regularly dispatched to the Midlands. It is for this purpose that carriage label boards 'Kingsbridge-Birmingham' were made. Similarly, crabs and lobsters were loaded out of Kingsbridge. These shell fish came mainly from Beesands, delivered in later years by Ned Stear.

At Brent in the autumn of each year there was a Sunday special working taking evergreen cut in the South Hams to the London and Birmingham flower markets.

During the pre-World War II period the South Hams was a popular holiday centre for the wealthy. Many owned luxury holiday villas dotted around the coastline and the hotels enjoyed a very high class of patronage. People with villas travelled down in the early summer and the various house parties brought passengers to the branch, whilst the parcels traffic to these villas was considerable, mostly coming from the principal London stores.

At weekends the through service to and from Paddington reached as many as 14 coaches on occasions. It is reported that a restaurant car was included, but it seems unlikely. Meanwhile the weekday working off the 'Riviera' could be two or three coaches.

The parcels traffic, luggage in advance etc., was quite heavy and the traffic in fish and rabbits was also considerable. As much as 25 tons of crabs and lobsters was loaded each week in 'Siphon Gs' or occasionally 'Siphon Cs'. These were despatched to London (Billingsgate), Birmingham and to Southampton for ocean liners. The Southampton traffic eventually went by road. Hallsands and Beesands fishermen were able to fish all the year round (except when easterly winds blew) whilst Lancombe, Salcombe and Hope Cove fishermen were only able to fish in the summer. In a good week there would be left, in the parcels office, a couple of choice crabs for the clerk and the porter. The Siphons usually left on either the 4.15 pm or 5.30 pm train.

Rabbits were a regular traffic for Birmingham and Sheffield, again in Siphons, loading up to 25 tons per week. This traffic normally left on the 2.05 pm train, the return working conveying live pigeons to Kingsbridge.

When the details were known i.e. destination, tonnage, train time and wagon number, the receiving centre was wired to enable sufficient road vehicles to be available to unload the rail vehicles on arrival.

The GWR first introduced camping coaches in 1934 and the branch was one of those selected for the location of sites. Sites were established at Avonwick, Gara Bridge and Loddiswell, so you can see the GWR thought there was distinct attraction and charm in this beautiful branch. At first the coaches were converted clerestory vehicles of three types. However only two types came to the branch.

A pannier tank arrives at Gara Bridge on an early morning train for Kingsbridge in the mid-1950s watched by lads using the camping coaches. *Ken Williams Collection*

Avonwick | Type 'A'. A vehicle with two berths at one end and four at the other with central kitchen alongside the four berths and a lounge/dining area.

Gara Bridge and Loddiswell | Type 'C'. A vehicle with access doors one side only. Looking at the door side, accommodation was as follows: 2 berth compartment, kitchen, lounge/dining room, four berths leading to two berths. In the corner of the lounge was a small cloak room with wash basin.

Toilet facilities were those provided at the local station as also was fresh water.

Both types were equipped for oil lighting, heating and cooking and the hire included bedding, table linen, cutlery, crockery, kitchen and cleaning utensils, stove and lamps and covered the period noon Saturday to am the following Saturday. The hire in 1934 was £3 per week for type 'A' and £5 per week for type 'C'. The rates remained fairly static, but a condition was that users of type 'A' bought four full monthly return fares and type 'C' six full monthly return fares and a non-returnable deposit of ten shillings was required. Tickets were required to be ordered when making the booking.

The branch allocation varied between three and six coaches over the years. Avonwick lost its coaches first and they all vanished at the end of the 1962 season. After nationalisation old toplight coaches were adapted and calor gas was installed in place of oil.

Cleanliness was always a problem with these vehicles. The company provided fresh linen each week and the station master was responsible for cleaning prior to each new letting. However, people were not always as tidy or clean as they might be. At Gara Bridge for example, two vehicles were normally stabled each summer and to ensure the vehicles met the company's standards, the afternoon signalman booked on four hours early on Saturdays to assist the station master with cleaning operations .

On one occasion, a swarm of bees settled in the lamp hut adjoining the camp coaches at Gara Bridge and had to be destroyed with cyanide gas. On another occasion bees swarmed in one of the cypress trees opposite the signal box. The local bee keeper was summoned and cut off the branch with the swarm on, and removed it.

It was always the intention to give a good service to the 'campers' and both Gara Bridge and Loddiswell staff worked hard to this end especially in the 1950s. Advance notice of the number of people coming and ages gave an indication of their needs, especially for children. At Gara Bridge a play area was set up for them - skittles, sand pit, swing, books etc. Even the delivery of groceries, milk, bread and the daily newspapers was arranged whilst flowers from the station gardens would decorate the inside of the coaches. One final touch of concern and interest was the kettle boiling ready for a 'cuppa' as the campers' train arrived at the respective stations.

It was not unknown for the occupants of the coaches to be invited to take baths in the homes of the station staff. Again this shows the enthusiasm of the Kingsbridge branch staff to help the customers.

Letters from contented visitors to the branch coaches were quite considerable and the authors have read some of those that have survived the years. The same people came year after year to the same site. A regular visitor to Gara Bridge was the Chairman of the British Road Services and his family.

At Gara Bridge many improvements to the facilities were added in the 1950s. When Plymouth streets were being relaid, the old stone sets were lifted for dumping. Several wagon loads arrived at Gara Bridge and found further use in the edging of the platforms and gardens around the camp coaches. This work was done by Ken Cornelius, Gordon Williams and John Watts. For the summer the whole area was greatly improved and brought a letter of commendation from the district traffic superintendent (Mr F.G. Dean).

In 1962 four vehicles again came to the branch - two at Gara Bridge and two at Loddiswell. The charge for the peak period 10th June to 2nd September was £12 per week and all the vehicles were eight berth. The season began on the 18th March and ended on 14th October. The qualification was again based on a minimum of six adult rail tickets.

The coaches were withdrawn at the end of the 1962 season and never returned. Some of the branch vehicles went to Dawlish Warren and survive (though no longer used), being owned by the Railway Staff Association. Gara Bridge featured in the last brochure prepared and published by BR, as it had so often done previously, and the bill poster, by an artist called Barber, was loosely based on the Gara Bridge site.

In 1957 a family stayed at Gara Bridge which resulted in an article being published in the Harrod's House Magazine written by Keith Bailey. The article sums up the spirit and attraction the coaches had for people and part is reproduced below:

> When we arrived at Gara Bridge we could appreciate the fact that it was little known because apart from the station and the station master's house, there was nothing except masses of scenery and, most important of all, the camping coach which was to be our home for two weeks. It stood on a siding behind the station and examination showed that it had everything we needed. Moreover, the station staff (station master and signalman) had the table laid for tea, bowls of flowers in the dining room and the kettle just on the boil!

> I must say that British Railways had thought of everything, the coach being fully equipped to meet the needs of eight persons. The dining room was spacious, light and airy and looked out on to a lawn on one side and the flowered covered station on the other. Sleeping accommodation was in single bunks, quite comfortable and fresh bed linen was supplied every week, as were table cloths and tea cloths, etc.

> I have said that Gara Bridge is not well known and having stayed there I hope it remains like that. It is the first place I have visited in Britain which has no drinking water, no electricity, no milk delivery and no newspapers. The water is brought by train from some four miles up the line and the electricity is not brought at all.

> One's shopping is performed via the signalman, who takes the order and phones it to the nearest village three miles away and what one has ordered comes up on the next train. Cooking is by oil and after using this for two weeks one wonders if the so-called benefits of civilisation in the shape of gas and electricity are of such benefit as one is led to believe.

In pre-war days the down 'Riviera' left Paddington at 10.30 am with six coaches for Penzance, a brake composite each for St Ives, Falmouth and Kingsbridge, a 60 ft slip (one of three 6962/3/4) brake composite for Minehead and a slip and brake composite for Weymouth. The Kingsbridge coach was detached at Exeter going forward at 1.37 pm. The return working was attached to the 11.25 from Kingswear joining the main train at Newton Abbot.

The 'B' sets were diagrammed to work as follows:

Set 1   7.20 am ex-Kingsbridge finishing at 3.20 pm with 4 round trips to Brent.
Set 2   2.0 pm ex-Kingsbridge finishing at 9.20 pm with 3 round trips to Brent.

Small standard GWR coach label boards were affixed with 'Brent' on one side and 'Kingsbridge' on the other.

During the Kingsbridge Fair week - usually around the 20th July - much cattle traffic was handled at the station and in pre-war days it would require two class '45XX' 2-6-2T locomotives to haul the trains away. As many as 120 wagons of livestock would be loaded and these were worked away as special trains, appearing only in the weekly working notices of extra and altered trains.

There were through wagons conveyed on Saturdays to Bristol for Burton-on-Trent as the empty beer casks etc. were returned to be refilled. On Tuesdays and Thursdays there were through vehicles to Paddington attached at Newton Abbot on the Penzance-Paddington freight. Normally the freights were worked from Plymouth to Newton Abbot calling at Brent around 2.45 pm, this connecting with the 12.20 pm (mixed) and 1.50 pm (freight) trains from Kingsbridge. The 11.50 am freight from the branch connected with the Ivybridge-Newton Abbot freight at Brent. Trains worked similarly in the reverse direction from Newton Abbot.

In the Autumn of 1941 sugar beet began to be loaded for shipment to sugar factories for processing. This trade built up quite rapidly and by the late 1950s as much as 100 tons per day were being despatched during the season.

The commencement of hostilities in 1939 meant the departure of many railwaymen into the armed forces and ladies were employed to take over some of their duties. However, the South Hams became a military area and much extra traffic was handled.

The Royal Navy set up establishments in Salcombe, Gara Rock and Thurlestone. The Royal Marines occupied the Thurlestone Hotel as a school for commissioning NCOs into the Corps. An establishment of *HMS Arethusa* was set up in Salcombe.

The Army set up several units in and around Kingsbridge mainly 'ack-ack' and coastal batteries, whilst the RAF had an air sea rescue unit at Salcombe, an aerodrome at Bolt Head, West Prawle and Hope Cove together with radio installations.

The busiest time ever on the branch was during the war with the evacuation of children from cities and the enormous amount of military traffic handled at all stations.

The evacuation of the Army from Dunkirk brought special trains with returning soldiers several coming to the South Hams to re-equip, recover from their ordeal and reorganise. The Northumberland Fusiliers and the Royal

BRENT AND KINGSBRIDGE

THE SPEED OF TRAINS OVER THE BRANCH MUST NOT EXCEED 35 MILES PER HOUR

Single Line, worked by Electric Train Token

Intermediate Crossing Place, Gara Bridge

Down Trains
Week Days only

Distance from Brent and M.P. Mileage M.C.	STATIONS	Ruling Gradient 1 in	Time Allowances for Freight Trains (See page 5) Point to Point Times Mins.	Allow for Stop Mins.	Allow for Start Mins.	B Mixed ‡ dep.	B Mixed SO (Not advertised) U dep.	K Freight SX dep.	B Pass SO dep.	B Pass SX dep.	G Engine SO dep.	B Mixed ‡ SX dep.	B Pass SO dep.	B Pass SO dep.	K Freight SX arr. / dep.	B Mixed SO K dep.	B Pass SO dep.	B Pass SX dep.	B Pass SO dep.	B Pass SO dep.	B Pass SX dep.	B Pass SO dep.	B Pass ¶ dep.	B Pass dep.
—	BRENT					a.m. 8V21	a.m. 8 5	a.m. 9 5	a.m. 9 25	a.m. 10 10	a.m. 11‖53	p.m. 12 24	p.m. 12 31	—	p.m. 1 50 / 2 5	p.m. 2 10	p.m. 3† 5	p.m. 4 15	p.m. 5 20	p.m. 5 35	p.m. 6 12	p.m. 7 0	¶	p.m. 9 20
2 43	Avonwick	50 F.	7	1	1	8 27	9 12	9 5	9 16	10 17	12‖53	12 31	12 34	1 59	2 17	2 17	3 40	4 15	5 27	5 42	6 19	7 7	7Q15	9 27
5 47	Gara Bridge	83 F.	8	—	1	8 36	9X24	9X24	9 25	10 25	CS	12X39	12X49	2 15	2X28	2X28	3 47	4X36	5X35	5X50	6X31	7Q7	7Q15	9 35
7 5	Topsham Crossing	110 F.	—	—	—	9X24	9a24	CR	X43	10 3	CS	12X39	12X49	X2 35	P3	—	3 55	4X33	5X35	5X50	6X31	—	—	—
8 72	Loddiswell	50 R.	9	1	1	8 44	9 32	10Ph3	10 33	—	—	12 47	12 57	1 44	2 53	2 36	4 3	4 41	5 43	5 58	6 39	7Q23	7Q23	9 43
10 64	Stop Board	50 F.	6	1	1	—	—	9d45X	—	—	—	—	—	1 55	P3 8	2 47	4 14	4 52	5 4	6 9	6 50	7Q34	7Q34	9 43
12 35	KINGSBRIDGE		5	1	—	8 55	9 43	10 10	10 44	10 44	12‖20	12 58	1 8	1 55	3 10	2 47	4 14	4 52	5 15	5 54	6 50	7Q34	9 54

Up Trains
Week Days only

Distance from Kingsbridge M.C.	STATIONS	Ruling Gradient 1 in	Time Allowances for Freight Trains (See page 62) Point to Point Times Mins.	Allow for Stop Mins.	Allow for Start Mins.	B Pass SUSPENDED SO dep.	B Pass SO dep.	B Pass SX dep.	B Pass SO dep.	B Pass SX dep.	B Freight SX arr. / dep.	B Pass SO dep.	C Empty SO dep.	B Pass SO dep.	B Pass SX dep.	B Mixed § SO dep.	B Mixed § SX dep.	C Empty Stock SO dep.	B Pass SO dep.	K Freight Pd421 dep.
—	KINGSBRIDGE					a.m. 7 27	a.m. 9 5	a.m. 9 25	a.m. 10N55	a.m. 11 15	a.m. 11 55 / 12 30	p.m. 12 30	p.m. 1†18	p.m. 2 10	p.m. 3† 5	p.m. 4 15	p.m. 5 15	p.m. 5 30	CS	p.m. 8 10
1 51	Stop Board	50 R.	6	1	1	7 27	9 5	9 35	11 7	11 25	12 3 / 12 11	12 40	—	2 20	—	4 25	5 25	5 40	—	8 0
3 43	Loddiswell	50 F.	3	1	1	7 37	9 16	9 35	11 15	11 33	12 11 / 12 20	12 30	X1250	2 38	4X57	4 48	5 43	5 58	CXS	8 35
5 30	Topsham Crossing	110 R.	8	1	1	7 45	9X23	9X43	C11‖25	11 23	X12 49	X1250	+36X	2X28	4X34	4X57	5 5	6 6	8 16	—
9 68	Gara Bridge	83 R.	7	1	1	7 53	9 31	9 61	11 27	11Y49	1 52	12 57	1†36X	2 38	4 42	5 5	5 43	6†47	6 24	8 51
9 72	Avonwick	50 R.	8	1	—	8 1	9 59	9 59	11 31	1 20	1 5	1 5	1 52	2 44	4 50	5 13	5 51	6 6	—	—
12 35	BRENT										1 37			3†37						

K—Conveys through coaches from Paddington (Brent arrive 3.11 p.m. See page 34). N—Through coaches to London, attached at Brent by Branch engine to rear of 11.15 a.m. Plymouth to Paddington (Brent 11.45-11.54 a.m. See page 74). O—To run ten minutes later throughout on Saturdays. U—To convey passengers unable to connect with 8.21 a.m. Brent and wagons with important traffic from Brent. V—On Saturdays not to be held more than five minutes for main line connections. Y—Engine to be released immediately, to leave at 11‖53 a.m. to Kingsbridge. Z—If 8.25 a.m. Paddington (due Brent 12.57 p.m.) running more than thirty minutes late, branch train to start punctually and passengers off London train to travel on 2.10 p.m. a—Arrive ten minutes earlier. A b—Arrive two minutes earlier. d—Arrive three minutes earlier. ‡—To convey wagons with important traffic only from Brent. §—To convey wagons from Kingsbridge to Brent only. ¶—(SX). 7.10 p.m. (SO) Brent not able to leave Gara Bridge by 7.40 p.m., 7.50 p.m. Kingsbridge to be sent away to time and cross the Down train at Gara Bridge. Truck of Cattle may be sent from Kingsbridge on any Passenger Train to Brent, at which station it will be transferred to a Freight Train.

Timetable for January 1941.

Welsh Fusiliers are known to have arrived.

Evacuation of schoolchildren played an important part in railway operations during the early war years. The thinking behind the various schemes was that young people would be moved away from possible enemy target areas e.g. cities, ports and industrial towns and live in the safer rural areas. In the event however Kingsbridge was attacked on several occasions by enemy aircraft.

During February 1941, schools in the Bristol area were evacuated to Devon and Cornwall. Those children and teachers fortunate to come to Kingsbridge boarded their trains at Bedminster station on the outskirts of Bristol. On 18th February the empty stock left Dr Days sidings at 10.20 am for Bedminster arriving at 10.35 with departure at 11.0 and carried 220 passengers. Stopping at Exeter St David's, Exeter St Thomas and Totnes, it eventually arrived at Brent at 2.10 pm where passengers boarded the branch train, arriving at Kingsbridge at 3.20 pm. The empty stock departed from Brent at 2.45 pm returning to Dr Days sidings. Both trains ran under class 'A' headlamps.

A similar train ran on the 19th February starting from Bristol Marsh Pond at 9.20 am arriving Bedminster at 9.35 am, leaving at 10.0 am. This time the train stopped at Exeter St David's and Newton Abbot where a portion for the Torquay branch was detached. Passengers for Kingsbridge were conveyed in the front four coaches, working direct to Kingsbridge and arriving at 1.55 pm. Again the empty stock was returned to Bristol joining the Torquay portion at Newton Abbot and running under class 'A' headlamps.

Both trains stopped at Newton Abbot for engine purposes on the outward journey away from platforms.

The London evacuation programme also included Kingsbridge. This time the Southern Railway was involved and a special was handed over to the GWR at Exeter St David's on two consecutive days leaving at 2.35 pm. There were 800 passengers on the first day and 200 on the second day. The GWR specials originated at Paddington and ran on two consecutive days departing at 2.40 pm with arrival at Kingsbridge at 8.30 pm - each train carrying 800 passengers, mainly from the Acton area.

The operation of these evacuation specials was closely co-ordinated with the company and local authorities. Station masters were to ensure that the specials, if possible, were watered, gassed and cleaned before the return journey of the empty stock commenced. With the arrival of these specials, the station master had to ensure all luggage was removed from the trains, the correct number of passengers were received and that they were handed over to the local reception officer. At the end of each day, a return had to be submitted to Divisional Office giving date, train reporting number, arrival time, loading point, and number of passengers. It was left to the station master to decide if ambulance staff would be required on arrival of the specials.

In early 1940 the '25th Animal Transport Company' of the Indian Army was billeted in the monastery at Woodleigh having arrived by rail at Loddiswell. Latterly the station was manned by a leading porter working a 7 hour 20 minute day, normally 7 am to 5.0 pm with a meal break in between.

When the water authority improved the water supply in the South Hams in the early 1950s Loddiswell yard was the main store for all the heavy steel pipes.

The porter - Alan Gidley - had the job of checking and recording the quantities moved so that the water company could be charged for the services rendered by the railway.

In the yard was also a rack for the storage of telegraph poles for the GPO. This was a main storage point for the area in addition to that at Kingsbridge. The cattle dock was used for the loading and unloading of cattle, but this traffic vanished by the mid-1950s. However, there was considerable traffic in Manitoba wheat ex-Avonmouth for Woodleigh Monastery which also, strangely enough, stored flour for the Royal Navy. This traffic also went by rail, mainly to Weymouth.

In 1943, with the evacuation of the Slapton area, terrific strain was placed on the railway. Firstly the area had to be evacuated of the civilian population to be followed by the incoming US army and navy. The first arrivals were the service corps to lay out and arrange barracks for the troops and to improve some roads for the use of armoured vehicles. Ammunition and explosives stores were set up at strategic points and the ammunition and explosives were brought in mainly by rail, unloading taking place at Gara Bridge, Loddiswell and Kingsbridge.

Many extra trains were run for the troops and the first train to arrive at Kingsbridge came from Gourock with US Navy personnel. Once in, the troops were given leave and a brisk trade in London tickets followed.

As training continued, so the inspections began by senior officers, culminating in visits by Generals Montgomery and Eisenhower. General Eisenhower's train, code name 'Alive', spent several days in Kingsbridge and was made up of GWR stock, including special saloons Nos. 9002 and 9113, and a wagon (Python) was included in the train for the General's giant American car. The General's departure from the station was quite formidable - surrounded by motor cycle outriders, the noise was enough to wake up the whole town.

There are two known visits by General Montgomery. His train, code name 'Rapier', came on both occasions from the Southern Railway and was made up of seven LNER vehicles and two LMS Python 'A's. 'Monty's' car also travelled with him in the train, but being a Rolls Royce, his departure was dignified and quiet and without outriders, just himself and his driver.

Both trains were hauled by two '45XX' class 2-6-2 tanks and to enable the engines to run round, the first locomotive was uncoupled at the home signal and the train ran into the station. When required, the second engine, having coupled up to the rear of the train, pulled the stock out to release the engine from the buffer stops.

'Monty' often took walks around Kingsbridge, usually on his own, quite unconcerned by his rank and position as Britain's most famous general and apparently oblivious of security. He always had a friendly word and greeting for the staff and locals.

Thanks to some records of Mr Baldwin the station master, we are able to record some of the various specials run during the post-training period at Slapton:

25th April, 1944	Train for RAF departed at 9.55 headed by 5551 to Moreton-in-Marsh. Made up of 2 GW and 2 LMS coaches with 3 LMS, 1 SR and 1 LNER van carrying 138 personnel.
29th April, 1944	Train for Lewes via Reading headed by 5519 with 116 personnel. Made up of 1 GW and 3 LMS coaches, 3 LNE, 2 SR and 4 LMS vans and 2 LMS open wagons.
29th April, 1944	Train from Eastbourne with 154 RAF personnel arrived 8.38 pm. 4 GW coaches, 7 LNE, 2 LMS vans and 1 SR brake van.
14th May, 1944	Train arrived 6.0 am at Kingsbridge with driver Aldridge, fireman Hine and guard Cox crew for US Army special. Made up of 9 LMS, 5 GW, 1 LNE vans, 1 LMS open and the Kingsbridge brake van.
15th May, 1944	Train of 14th May left at 3.29 am to US Army, North Savernake, loaded with ammunition. The crew being driver Dunn, fireman Canham and guard Cox.

The crew of this train came back with engine and brake van very promptly for at 5.47 am they again left with a similar train (15 wagons only) for North Savernake. Again a quick return and they were ready for the first up train of the day.

| 14th May, 1944 | Combined RN and US Navy train from Appledore (SR), with 294 RN and 176 US Navy personnel for Salcombe. A twelve coach train - 11 LMS, 1 GW. During transit 5 windows and 1 ventilator were broken whilst a compartment glass door (GW) was lost. |

This was a busy weekend on the branch as you can see from the above movements. On the Sunday the US Army loaded 39 wagons with ammunition between Sunday 4.30 pm and 1.30 am on the Monday. However, when the station staff checked the yard on the Monday morning they found ten boxes of grenades, a crate of 60 shells and 22 rounds of high explosive and six canisters containing 75 mm gun barrels left on the ground!!

16th May, 1944	Combined train for RAF (85 personnel) and US Army (219 personnel). 4 GW and 5 LMS coaches. 1 LNE, 1 LMS, van. The RAF were destined for Swansea and the US Army for Dorchester and left early am. At 11.00 am the two branch 'B' sets were used to Brent with an SR van attached to take 66 RAF personnel to Helston.
22nd May, 1944	Extra coach full first for 32 Royal Marines from Thurlestone attached to the 'B' set.
30th May, 1944	Down freight arrived with 11 wagons, 6 coal, 2 beer from Burton, 1 manure ex-Avonmouth, 2 lubricating oil for RAF.

In the midst of all this military traffic, a 'Siphon C' was loaded with fish for London on the 5.30 pm train. Normal services still had to run and the strain on the staff is obvious from the foregoing.

At Gara Bridge to enable the Saturday through train to run non-stop to Brent a system was set up whereby the station master stood at the Kingsbridge end of the station to take the Kingsbridge-Gara Bridge token. The signalman could see if it was safely received and handed over the Brent token to the fireman by the signal box. This saved time and coal and kept the trains moving. There are no recorded failures of this system.

BRENT AND KINGSBRIDGE (FOR SALCOMBE). (Week Days only.)

	a.m.	p.m	p.m		p.m.		p.m	p.m	p.m			a.m.	a.m.	a.m.		p.m	p.m		p m	p m		p m
Brent ..... dep.	8 25	12 24	4 15	...	5 20	...	7 0	8 50	9 40	**Kingsbridge**												
Avonwick . ,,	8 32	12 31	4 22	...	5 27	...	7 7	8 57	9 47	(for Salcombe) dep.	7 33	...	9 50	...	11 0	...	12 30	2 10	...	4 15	5 15	...	7 45
Gara Bridge ... ,,	8 40	12 38	4 32	...	5 35	...	7 15	9 5	9 55	Loddiswell ,,	7 43	...	9 40	...	11 10	...	12 30	2 20	...	4 25	5 25	...	7 55
Loddiswell . ,,	8 48	12 47	4 41	...	5 43	...	7 23	9 13	10 3	Gara Bridge ... ,,	7 50	...	9 47	...	11 17	...	12 38	2 27	...	4 33	5 33	...	8 3
Kingsbridge										Avonwick ,,	7 59	...	9 56	...	11 26	...	12 47	2 36	...	4 42	5 42	...	8 11
(for Salcombe) arr.	9 0	12 53	4 52	...	5 55	...	7 35	9 24	10 14	Brent ...... arr.	8 7	...	10 5	...	11 35	...	12 56	2 45	...	4 50	5 51	...	8 19

F—For Brean Sands and Lympsham.
G—Saturdays excepted.
H—By Western National Bus to St. Austell (heavy luggage not conveyed.)

K—Bristol (Temple Meads) depart 6.25 p.m. (via Badminton).
P—By Western National Bus to St. Erth (heavy luggage not conveyed).
S—Saturdays only. V—Via Westbury.
W—Wednesdays and Saturdays only. Q—Third class only.

January 1947 timetable

Summer 1952 timetable

Table 92   BRENT and KINGSBRIDGE (for Salcombe)

Week Days only

	a.m	a.m	p.m	p.m	p.m	p.m	p.m	p.m	p.m	p.m	p.m		
	S	**E**	**S**	**S**	**S**	**SE**	**E**	**S**	**E**	**S**			
Brent .... dep	8 20	9 48	12 24	12 34	1 20	2 10	3 40	4 15	4 40	5 20	5 35	6 10 7 0	9 20	**B** Through Carriages from London (Paddington) dep. 10 55 a.m. (Tables 61 and 81)
2½ Avonwick	8 27	9 54	12 30	12 40	1 27	2 17	3 47	4 22	4 47	5 27	5 42	6 17 7 7	9 27	
6½ Gara Bridge............	8 35	10 2	12 38	12 48	1 35	2 27	3 54	4 32	4 55	5 35	5 50	6 27 7 15	9 35	**S** Saturdays only
9 Loddiswell	8 43	10 10	12 46	12 56	1 43	2 35	4 34	4 41	5 3	5 43	5 58	6 36 7 23	9 43	**E** Except Saturdays
12½ Kingsbridge .... arr	8 55	10 25	12 58	1 8	1 55	2 50	4 15	4 52	5 15	5 55	6 10	6 50 7 35	9 54	**Z** Through Carriages to London (Paddington) arr. 4 12 p.m. (Tables 81 and 61)

Week Days only

	a.m	a.m	a.m	a.m	a.m	a.m	non		p.m	p.m	p.m	p.m	p.m	p.m	
	S	**E**	**S**	**SZ**	**E**	**S**			**S**	**E**	**S**	**S**	**E**	**S**	
Salcombe ¶ ...... der	6 55	6 55	8 30	10 0	10 30	10 30	12 0	..	1 30	3 30	4 0	4 30	5 0	7 0	**¶** By Western National Omnibus (6 miles). Road Services are also operated from Kingsbridge to Thurlestone and Hope
Kingsbridge .... dep	7 27	7 33	9 5	10 55	11 0	11 15	12 30	..	2 10	4 15	4 38	5 15	5 30	7 50	
3½ Loddiswell	7 37	7 43	9 15	..	11 10	11 25	12 40	..	2 20	4 25	4 48	5 25	5 40	8 0	
7 Gara Bridge..............	7 44	7 50	9 22	..	11 17	11 32	12 48	..	2 27	4 33	4 56	5 33	5 48	8 8	
10 Avonwick..............	7 53	7 59	9 30	..	11 25	11 40	12 56	..	2 35	4 42	5 4	5 42	5 57	8 15	
12½ Brent.............. arr	8 1	8 7	9 40	11 30	11 35	11 50	1 5	..	2 45	4 50	5 15	5 51	6 6	8 24	

Another time saving feature was that the down through train stopped at Gara Bridge and the station master then travelled on the train to collect tickets saving passengers valuable time on arrival at Kingsbridge. A considerable effort was needed to collect some 300 tickets in about 20 minutes.

When the station master - Mr K. Cornelius - left in 1956, the station house became vacant and was not used again as a residence by BR staff.

During the winter 1954/5 severe weather set in. On 4th January, 1955 heavy falls of snow closed roads and caused a token failure between Gara Bridge and Kingsbridge. Derek Wilson - Kingsbridge signalman - set off to walk to Gara to commence pilot working. The snow was treacherous and Derek continued to trudge on through deep drifts. Eventually, he arrived at Gara very tired, and cold and then piloted the train - the last of the day - to Kingsbridge. He was subsequently commended by the railway for his efforts.

Derek featured in yet another commendation in 1957. Sitting in Kingsbridge box on the evening of 28th July, he heard what sounded like a train approaching. No train was scheduled and no train had been offered by Gara Bridge. Suddenly, he saw a Permanent Way trolley hurtle out of the cutting with some youths on board. Taking prompt action, Derek switched the king point to the goods yard and eventually the trolley - minus youths - crashed into the goods shed. It transpired that some holiday youngsters found the trolley near Sorley and broke the locks. For a bit of fun they placed it on the line not realising the gradient and they and the trolley took off towards Kingsbridge.

The Permanent Way gang of Loddiswell were a keen bunch of railwaymen, and proud of 'their' line. So much so that in 1959 they were rewarded by winning the award for the best kept length of track in Plymouth Division.

An incident occurred one evening with the night engineman. As detailed in Chapter Seven, his duties were quite involved and on his ability depended the first train of the day. Now the night engineman was authorised to move the engine on shed only. However, water was normally taken from the crane near to the signal box and usually the late turn signalman left the catch point pulled so that access was available to the crane from the shed. However, one night the signalman went off duty failing to set the point. The inevitable happened. Needing to water the engine, the night man climbed the footplate and opened the regulator and set off. Bang!! Crash!! Through the catch point and into the bank with all wheels off the track! No early morning train that day, but the breakdown train was summoned from Laira, and buses were used to take passengers on their journeys.

With the arrival of Mr F.G. Dean in Plymouth as district traffic superintendent, the encouragement of station staff was sought in keeping the station tidy. Throughout the district more and more stations entered the station garden competitions and Kingsbridge fell in with this scheme quite happily. Avonwick, Gara Bridge and Loddiswell invariably had attractive gardens. Prizes were won and competition was keen. Cleanliness was not confined to just the platform area. Many a staff member was surprised by Mr Dean opening cupboards and looking behind doors to ensure that all was clean and tidy.

Finally, to conclude this chapter is a table showing the known types of locomotives, diesel railcars, coaches, branch goods brake van and shed allocation of Newton Abbot (engines suitable for the branch only) which supplied power for the branch.

There may have been others which are not included - certainly for the period 1893-1924, which the authors have not been able to establish. The goods vehicles and through vehicle workings could have used any standard company vehicle whilst goods stock from all companies came onto the branch.

Engines
GWR Locomotives

0-6-0 '2251' class	2211
2-6-2T '31XX' class	3101 and 3104 later renumbered 4401 and 4404
2-6-2T '45XX' class	4516, 4550, 4555, 4561, 4568, 4570 4577, 4582, 5519, 5525, 5533, 5544, 5551, 5557, 5558, 5564, 5568, 5573
0-4-2T '517' class	Numbers unknown
0-6-0PT '57XX' class	3796, 9633, 9678
0-6-0PT	2062

BR Steam Locomotives
2-6-2T   82006, 82009, 82029, 82033

BR Diesel Locomotives   D6301, D6303, D6310, D6319, D6329, D6339, D6330, D6333,
North British   D6334, D6338, D6342, D6345 (with snow plough)
Diesel Hydraulic
'D63XX' class

BR Diesel Railcars
Single units.
'55000' class   W55000, W55001, W55006, W55009, W55010, W55011, W55014,
                          W55015, W55016, W55017, W55019, W55034
Two car set   W50922 / W50869
Three car set   W51145 / W59034 / W51132

Coaches GWR
'B' set labelled Kingsbridge No. 1   6453 / 6454
'B' set labelled Kingsbridge No. 2   6968 / 6969
Non branded   6335 / 6336
                                        6443 / 6444
                                        6640 / 6641
Single Coaches Brake 1st / 3rd   6278
Single Coaches Brake 1st / 3rd   6284

Goods brake van
16 ton labelled Kingsbridge   35662

Camping Coaches
                    Gara Bridge   *Loddiswell*
Toplight   9952   9891
Clerestory   9909

Shed Allocation of classes which could have used the branch. Newton Abbot (NA) BR 83A.

March 1938	4540	4574	5505	5567	5798		
	4542	4587	5552		9717		
	4547	5501	5557				

1947	4405	4516	4582	5530	5557	5798	9717
		4526	4587	5551		9623	
		4547	5505	5552		9633	

Chapter Six

Boats and Buses

Although not the main concern of this book, a book about the South Hams would not be complete without reference to the river traffic and the road motor omnibuses. The GWR took over the river services to Salcombe in the late 1920s and of course were responsible for the introduction of buses to the area.

As has already been stated, there was a flourishing ship building industry at Kingsbridge and boats have always had a fascination for 'land lubbers.' The locals took to using the river for both business and some pleasure and it was soon apparent that there was a living to be made plying the waters of the estuary.

There were two services operating from Kingsbridge to cater for the traffic being offered. The first was the Plymouth service, calling at Salcombe, begun in 1857, whilst the Salcombe service followed as late as 1906.

The first boat was called the *Kingsbridge Packet* and was owned and operated by Hurrell Anthony Beer & Co. Robert Hurrell realised the opportunities in shipping and persuaded local business men to invest in the company. Needless to say the majority were men who could offer traffic to the company. The *Kingsbridge Packet* was built locally being a wooden paddle boat and launched in 1857. Weighing 69 tons gross she operated a twice-weekly service to Plymouth calling at Salcombe in both directions with a daily service to Salcombe, all of course dependent upon tides.

There was no competition for many years until a former shareholder, William Heath Prowse, decided to set up a rival company with premises in Salcombe in 1879. Mr Prowse was a brewer in Kingsbridge. Probably to annoy his rivals, he called his ship the *King's Bridge Packet*, having her built by Harveys of Hayle, Cornwall. Not content with having a similar name, the vessel had to be larger and was of 110 tons gross, an iron screw-driven vessel with compound engines.

The opposition panicked at this new rival and ordered a new ship to be called the *South Hams Trader* - built at South Shields. However, before taking delivery, the company - Hurrell Anthony & Beer - went bankrupt and the Admiralty Marshal seized the *Kingsbridge Packet* and offered it for sale. The redoubtable Robert Hurrell bought the ship and continued trading on his own.

In 1883, Robert Hurrell died and his son John Squire Hurrell, the man who welcomed the GWR to Kingsbridge, took over operation of the vessel. Whilst operating the company, the son also assisted in the building of a vessel, again a wooden paddle boat, at the yard of Date & Sons, Kingsbridge. This new vessel, called *Express*, entered service in 1885, making three vessels operating the same Plymouth service. Obviously trade was sufficient to keep them all occupied until the arrival of the railway.

The original *Kingsbridge Packet* was broken up in 1890 whilst the *Express* was sold in 1894 to King and Pitts of Plymouth, being eventually sunk by a German submarine in 1915. With the demise of the *Kingsbridge Packet*, William Prowse renamed his vessel the *Kingsbridge Packet* and continued sailing until 1908 when

Ilton Castle approaching Kingsbridge.   *Cookworthy Museum*

Ilton Castle passes South Pool Creek with a Kingsbridge-bound ferry. We trust the occupants of the rowing boat survived the wash.   *Cookworthy Museum*

she was sold to a Humber operator.

The replacement vessel was built by Cox of Falmouth, again named *Kingsbridge Packet*, being a steel screw vessel of 128 tons gross. In the 1914/18 war the company name was changed to the Kingsbridge Packet Company and continued operations and service to the local community.

The other company which operated the Kingsbridge-Salcombe service was run by Nicholas March and Captain Nicholas Southwood. In 1906 Willoughby Brothers of Plymouth built a steel paddle boat of 53 tons gross called the *Ilton Castle* which was employed in operating daily sailings to and from Salcombe, with the occasional excursion trip to Torbay. The company prospered, although Nicholas March died in 1912 leaving his widow to continue the operations with his partner. So successful was the operation that in 1914 a second vessel was added called the *Kenwith Castle*, being built in the same yard and to the same design as its sister ship. However, as recorded later in the chapter, the GWR had begun bus operations in 1909 with a Kingsbridge-Salcombe service serving the local communities of West Alvington and Malborough but with no apparent ill effect on river operations at first.

With the improvement of road surfaces, smoother riding buses and a more reliable service, the bus soon became the scourge of the river operators, and traffic began to fall away, going to the bus and to some extent the car. In 1927 the vessels were sold to the GWR and Mrs March and Captain Southwood were glad to be rid of the liability.

The GWR were not keen to develop this new found asset and soon sold out of service, first the *Ilton Castle* as a house boat for Salcombe Yacht Club, then in 1932 the *Kenwith Castle* was sold to Southampton operators, and this was the end of large vessels using the quay.

It is perhaps pertinent to consider why the silting up of the river occurred.

For many years, schooners and sailing ships were busy at the quay loading and unloading cargoes with relatively few navigational problems. However, with the advent of the paddle steamer and screw-driven vessels, the natural bed and banks of the river were disturbed with the pressure and backwash from these power-driven vessels. Erosion of the banks caused silt to be stirred up and as a result mud banks became a hazard until the river eventually became unnavigable to larger vessels.

Salcombe came into its own again in World War II. The Royal Navy and American Navy filled the port and its bays with an armada of craft in preparation for, and in the operation of, Overlord - the invasion of Europe. All sorts of landing craft were to be seen in the port and needless to say the Devon people felt they were being invaded when they had to act as host to all the sailors.

Thus Salcombe became an anchorage for part of the vast armada of small invasion craft for D-Day on 6th June, 1944. In fact part of the South Hams was evacuated for training purposes of the various units, Slapton Sands being similar to the area of Normandy which was known as Omaha Beach. With the use of live ammunition, casualties were inevitable. The United States have erected a monument to the citizens who left their homes and farmsteads during this time; this stands in the middle of the beach. A full account of the

Kenwith Castle leaving Salcombe with a full complement of passengers for Kingsbridge.

Cookworthy Museum

Dates Yard, Kingsbridge with *Kenwith Castle* about to sail for Salcombe *c.* 1928.

Ken Williams Collection

evacuation of the South Hams will be found in Grace Bradbeer's book *The Land Changed Its Face*, published by David & Charles.

We now look at the public road services. We have already referred to the coach services which operated when the station at Kingsbridge Road (Wrangaton) was opened, leaving from the Kings Arm's, Kingsbridge to the new station at Kingsbridge Road. This service was operated by Messrs Foale and Tucker and ran three trips each way daily.

Similarly there was the service which ran from the Anchor Hotel, Kingsbridge to Dartmouth, this giving a rail link via the Kingswear branch.

These two coach services provided the main means of transport within the district for a number of years. Indeed with the opening of the railway in 1893, there were advertised road / rail / river excursions incorporating the River Dart steamers. One such excursion was Plymouth to Kingsbridge by rail, coach to Dartmouth, steamer to Totnes returning by rail to Plymouth for an inclusive fare of 5s. 6d.. If one wished one could spend two days over the excursion by staying overnight at a hotel, making a 'mini-holiday'. There was also a 5s. trip from Kingsbridge by rail to Dartmouth and coach to Kingsbridge, or you could do this trip in reverse.

As early as 1897, the GWR progressive and pioneering in so many ways throughout its history, was looking at the possible use of road transport in the development of its network of railways. Previously the trend in further development was in the use of light and narrow gauge railways. However, the motor vehicle had the advantages of (1) considerably less capital outlay; (2) lower working costs; (3) elasticity of movement in not being confined to a fixed track, which, in the case of light railways, was usually a single line.

As a beginning a trial was given in the Birmingham district to the use of motor vehicles for goods collection and delivery work. The experiment was not a success, largely owing to traders' objections and to waste of time in loading and unloading, thus preventing the vehicles being worked to the best advantage. It was then decided to experiment with passenger motor vehicles.

Developments took a turn for the better when the GWR decided to operate a public road vehicle from Helston to the Lizard a service which was inaugurated on 17th August, 1903. Four days before the service began, at the half-yearly meeting of the company, Lord Cawdor, the Chairman, had said:

We have also been considering the cases in which independent persons run motor-car services along the roads to our railway stations. We do not see why we should not feed our own railway ourselves by means of motor cars. We have, therefore, given instructions for the purchase of five motors which will each carry twenty-two passengers. They will be petrol motors. They will be capable of going at a moderate speed. There are various places where we think we can try them as feeders to our system, and it will be better that this means of conveyance should be in our own hands than in the hands of others. We shall be able to give convenience to the public in places where it is wanted, and we shall be in a position to find out what traffic there is in the district. When we find that out we shall then be in a position to determine whether it is a place suitable for a light railway, and whether there is any traffic which will pay. We are purchasing at present five of these motor cars, and I do not put it higher than an experiment which we think it wise to try. It is not a heavy expenditure, and the

Ilton Castle and *Kenwith Castle* at Salcombe *c*. 1905.   *Cookworthy Museum*

AEC bus No. T 8148 *c*. 1920, this vehicle was converted to a lorry in 1926 and was withdrawn in 1933.   *Ken Williams Collection*

convenience will be that if the motor car does not succeed in one place we can take it to another. The first car will be run shortly from Helston to The Lizard. There has been one light railway sanctioned there, if not more, but there has been always a failure to get the money (at least £85,000 was the estimate). The money is not there, but by putting a motor car on the route we shall find out what the traffic amounts to. If it does not pay we shall take it away and put it on elsewhere. It is hoped the proprietors will appreciate that these are experiments, in our view, in the right direction to keep ourselves up-to-date, and try to feed our own undertaking, and give convenience to the public.

Great difficulty was experienced in estimating the potential traffic to be obtained from any given area when setting up these early services.

Countings were taken of the number of people using the road, and particulars obtained of the populations served, but until some considerable experience had been obtained of the 'travelling habits' of the country people in different parts of England the results obtained were unreliable. For example, the services in Somerset (Cheddar and Bridgwater area) ran through an almost continuous line of houses and the roads generally were much used, but motor services could not be made to pay. On the other hand, the Llandyssil-New Quay service ran through miles of apparently empty moorland, but the service was one of the heaviest, the cars being usually full, passengers joining and leaving at every cross road.

The Road Motor Services were primarily run as feeders to the railway, and not with the idea of bringing in any large direct profit.

This fact was always borne in mind in working the services, and the amount of traffic brought to the railway by any special or regular trip was considered of more importance than if the trip was directly profitable in its own account. It was also taken into account in comparing the results of some of the private bus companies with the railway services.

In the area served by the GWR the most important centres, whether agricultural or manufacturing, were served direct by railway, and those districts which had no railway communication had either insufficient business to justify railway enterprise or were isolated by the fact that they did not lie on the direct route of a main or branch line.

In such cases, where the population was at all considerable, or the district had any possibility of traffic development, schemes for the provision of light railways had naturally suggested themselves, but for the reasons mentioned previously had not usually materialised. Amongst the other useful purposes which the road motor vehicles served was that of demonstrating the value from a traffic point of view of districts which had been represented as only waiting for the construction of a railway to develop and prosper.

The motor services stretching out from the termini of branch lines greatly extended the area from which passengers and parcels could be collected, and encouraged people living in remote country districts to travel.

As the cars also conveyed parcels and packages of goods up to 1 cwt per package, farmers and others, taking advantage of the cheap rates and special facilities introduced, were enabled to send their produce to new markets, and new areas of supply were opened to the public.

A fine view of bus No. T 8148 in the yard at Kingsbridge on 17th March, 1925. Note the solid tyres and Hackney Carriage plate. *GWR*

AEC bus No. BH 0274 was slightly more modern than T 8148. Vehicles of this type could also be found at Kingsbridge. *Western National*

When the motor services first started, following the usual railway practice the mechanical side was supervised from Swindon and the traffic arrangements from Paddington and by the local officers.

This system led to a large amount of duplication of work, delay, and considerable expense, and therefore when the first few cars had proved satisfactory and an extension of the services was decided upon, a separate department was formed to deal with both the traffic and mechanical sides. This system was the only suitable one for the motor work, as the duties of everyone connected with the department were so varied. The driver had to help with luggage, give information to passengers, distribute bills, arrange special trips, give information to management on service results and trip workings, and in some cases collect the fares. Conductors had to help with cleaning, handle the scotch, start the engine and help in case of failures.

In the early days of the services, drivers had to be drawn from private car work, and generally these men proved thoroughly unsatisfactory. Subsequently, nearly all the men employed had been trained by the department, and in most cases were employed by the company in some other capacity before they joined the motor department. Later, drivers received the whole of their training in the department, starting either as lad cleaners or conductors at the age of fifteen or as cleaners at eighteen. Whilst cleaning they learned to be thoroughly familiar with the cars, being allowed to drive from the shed to the washstand and to manoeuvre the cars about the yards. They also had the opportunity of picking up quite a large amount of mechanical knowledge and the use of tools, as they acted as 'fitters' mates' to the leading drivers. At the age of 19 or 20 the embryo driver was sent out conducting for two years. This work taught him to be clean, and also civil to passengers; he also helped with any failures which may have occurred on the road. His next step was to that of cleaner-driver, when in addition to cleaning, he acted as relief driver for meal times and on busy days. Then, as a vacancy occurred he took charge of a parcels van or goods lorry, and finally was promoted to regular passenger work.

Along with all the other developments within the GWR system, the company considered the South Devon area as a potential road motor car centre; in particular the South Hams. However, the South Hams did have a service operated from Modbury, in 1904, the South Hams Motor Carriers Ltd. But the GWR bought this company out in 1905 and it became the basis of its Plymouth area operations. At the same time development of services began in the Paignton area, encompassing Brixham, Dartmouth and Totnes.

To continue its expansion of road services, the company began a Kingsbridge-Salcombe service in July 1909 with a car based at Kingsbridge and one at Salcombe. Traffic was slow at first, but soon settled down to a steady and regular pattern and the fleet began to increase. Between 1911 and 1913 a service ran on Saturdays from Modbury to Salcombe via Kingsbridge, but no further additional routes were sought until after World War I.

With troops coming back from the war experienced in motor transport and the large quantities of motor vehicles available, the GWR looked at further developments at Kingsbridge. So much so that from July 1919 regular services commenced to Dartmouth and in 1920 this service was extended westwards to Yealmpton giving a through service Dartmouth-Yealmpton, only to be extended in 1921 to Plymouth. At this time the through service began (July 1921) Dartmouth-Salcombe, whilst in 1922 a service, summer Sundays only, was begun to Totnes and Newton Abbot.

The GWR used Milnes Daimlers quite extensively at the beginning of their bus operations. As a result an engineer - Mr Evans - was persuaded to join the GWR from Milnes Daimler. The family tradition continued when his son, W. Evans, was apprenticed to the Road Motor Department.

By happy coincidence, Mr Evans moved to Kingsbridge in the early 1920s as fitter-driver. At the same time several other drivers moved to Kingsbridge including Jack Martin, Jack Payne and Gordon Reid who lodged with the Miss Goss's in Fore Street, and a firm friendship sprang up between these young men.

Work was hard and hours long so every opportunity to relax was taken. These friends were regular worshippers at church on Sundays. However, some members of the congregation were upset at the end of worship when these fellows marched across to the 'local' for a pint. So much so that the parishioners complained to the Vicar about the drinking habits of the men from the GWR. The Vicar listened kindly and then spoke to our friends suggesting they wait behind next Sunday. As arranged the group met the Vicar after the service and as the congregation had gone they all went to the 'local' after which the Vicar invited them all back for supper. This was to be a regular occurrence for some time.

Working on the road cars was not done under ideal conditions - repairs often being done in the open. Breakdowns occurred from time to time and breakdown crews would be sent out. On one occasion a car broke down whilst climbing up to Churchstow from Aveton Gifford. The roads being narrow, the only way the car could be rescued was by the breakdown vehicle - another car - towing the cripple backwards up the hill. Not an easy job at night-time in the narrow lanes.

The evening car service to Plymouth connected with the night mail to the North and also provided a later service back to Kingsbridge. This was a service which was required to run at all costs. One afternoon the regular driver - Sid Camp - was unable to report for duty because his wife had had a baby that day. The fitter-driver - W. Evans - stepped in to run the service. However on the way fog set in and the car was slowed considerably. Approaching Flete Lodge a lantern was being waved at the driver who stopped. It appeared that Lord Mildmay of Flete - a Director of the company - had to travel to London that night and the road car was his only means of getting to Plymouth. Every effort was made to get through the fog to make the connection whilst his Lordship sat up with the driver. Happily he caught his train and rewarded the driver handsomely.

One Sunday our band of friends decided to have a day out at Torcross. They hired a wagonette from the Anchor Hotel and set off at 8 o'clock on their journey. However they came to an abrupt stop outside the Inn in Frogmore and the horse refused to go any further. The licensee and his wife watched the proceedings with great amusement and then let the travellers into the joke. The horse normally worked for the Post Office and this was a regular stopping point for the postman to deliver mail whilst the horse was given a bucket of beer. A drink all round - including the horse - resolved the situation so off they set again. Stopping at each pub they arrived at the Torcross Hotel just in time for lunch at 1 o'clock.

This tale does not end there. Whilst having lunch, two young army officers on a nearby table were discussing how to pay their bill. Mr Evans hearing this discussion approached the hotel proprietor who advised him that these officers had a broken down Argyl car in the garage worth about £20. A quick discussion amongst our friends resulted with an offer to purchase the car for £20 which was accepted. Thinking that the car could be towed back by the wagonette, they set off for Kingsbridge but the car had to be abandoned until it could be properly towed back. After repair it gave several years of good service.

Services were allowed to settle down, because of the lack of money arising out of a serious financial situation within the country at the time. However, July 1924 saw the introduction of a service to Thurlestone and one to Hope Cove - whilst the Sunday service to Newton Abbot ran all the year round.

By 1925 traffic was good and prosperous and further growth took place. A regular service to Totnes was started and new ground was opened with services to Torcross and East Portlemouth. The Salcombe service was still well used and was causing grave financial problems to the river. Through increased booking on the trains Salcombe became a popular resort.

Over the ensuing years additional services were commenced, a market day service to Dartmouth via Halwell (1926), Kingsbridge to Loddiswell and finally a service to South Pool (1928).

With all these services having been added over the years, a comprehensive network was established. The table below gives the routes and dates when services began.

Service		Opened
Kingsbridge-Salcombe		21.7.1909
Modbury-Kingsbridge-Salcombe		14.10.1911
Dartmouth-Kingsbridge-Salcombe		11.7.1921
Dartmouth-Kingsbridge		30.6.1919
Dartmouth-Kingsbridge-Modbury-Yealmpton		11.7.1920
Dartmouth-Kingsbridge-Plymouth		25.3.1921
	Split to 2 parts	9.2.1928
Kingsbridge-Totnes-Newton Abbot (Summer Sundays only)		4.6.1922
Kingsbridge-Totnes-Newton Abbot (Sunday only)		1.6.1924
Kingsbridge-Totnes (Daily)		13.7.1925
Kingsbridge-Totnes-Haytor (Sunday only)	18.7.1926 to	19.9.1926
Kingsbridge-Thurlestone		17.7.1924
Kingsbridge-Hope Cove		18.7.1924
Kingsbridge-East Portlemouth		26.11.1925
Torcross-East Portlemouth		13.7.1925

In August 1928 the railways obtained comprehensive powers for their road cars and used these to come to terms with provincial operators by either buying shares in existing companies or amalgamating with them to form new companies. As a result, in January 1929, the Western Omnibus Company Ltd came into being and all the Kingsbridge services were transferred to this new company. Many of the staff elected to go with the new operator, but retained their railway privileges and concessions. Because the staff were railwaymen, needless to say they remained members of the National Union of Railwaymen and today most of the depots of the Western National remain NUR strongholds.

The staff uniforms consisted of leather cap, jerkin waistcoat, breeches, gaiters, and a great coat, rather heavy wear but remember drivers in early days had no protection from the elements. Conductors carried a ticket punch and rack, and a large bag for fares collected. For the summer, dustcoats were issued. The crews were the responsibility of the station master and all monies collected were handed in to the booking office. Also schedules and time keeping were his concern. Tickets used were of the bell punch type, initially showing various locations on the routes concerned, but soon became plain numerical, reducing the number required to be stocked and a considerable saving on printing.

The liveries of the vehicles were the traditional coach colours of the company, using standard transfers where possible. There was a period prior to World War I when the cars were painted green (perhaps locomotive green).

The Salcombe service was always busy on summer Saturdays. The through train from London was well patronised and all road crews had to report for duty, providing up to ten duplicate services. Needless to say, this brought considerable strain on the operators of the day. Those people coming in one Saturday needed to be taken home the next week.

Excursions were always a popular feature of the GWR, and plenty of passengers came to see the glories of Devon. In 1927 Swindon Works had an outing to Salcombe and the whole fleet of road cars was lined up to meet the train. When Great Western handed over their South Hams fleet to the Western National the railway and buses were co-ordinated and rail connections were maintained. This co-ordination regrettably ceased from 1932 and has never occurred on a regular basis since.

A fuller history of all GWR road services can be found in John Cummings book *Railway Motor Buses and Bus Services in the British Isles 1902-1933* published by the Oxford Publishing Company.

Chapter Seven

The Running of the Station

There has been little attempt to outline the running of a station and with Kingsbridge we have the ideal opportunity to have an insight into the workings of a railway station. Kingsbridge was a Class 2 station. Before describing the duties of the various departments/staff perhaps it is worth recording the station staff of Kingsbridge in 1944 and to list the complete branch staff for the period 1958-1960.

Kingsbridge Staff 1944

Station Master	I. Baldwin
Chief Goods Clerk	E. Mitchell
Goods Clerks	Miss B. Nicholls, Miss L. Pears, Mrs D. Bailey, C. Ford
Parcel Clerk	P. Hawkes
Booking Clerks	L. Hanson Powter, D. Sutton
Guards	F. Viles, J. Cox
Shunter	W. Adams
Signalmen	A. Southcott, J. Cazley
Checker	R. Ball
Parcel Porter	W. Thomas
Mileage Porter	Mrs F. Clifton
Goods Porter	W. Edwards
Grade 2 Porters	A. Steer, W. Gidley, Mrs E. Peck, Miss M. Tucker, W. Wonnacott Snr
Motor Drivers	W. Wonnacott Jnr, W. Husband
Working Foreman	Provided by divisional relief

Salcombe

Clerk	Mrs E. Nicholson
Motor Driver	C. Patey
Motor Guard	M. Friend

There was a clerk employed as holiday relief between July-September inclusive.

Branch Staff in late 1958 and 1959

Kingsbridge

Station Master	H. Cox
Chief Clerk (Goods)	E. Mitchell
Clerks	J. Barnes, J. Hughes, R. Friend
Booking Office/Parcels	D. Batten, B. Braund, E. Gillard
Porters	E. Evans, R. Edmonds, R. Collins, M. Edmonds, F. Husband, H. Gillard
Shunter/Guards	J. Cox, K. Jerred, W. Innes
Carriage Cleaner	F. Elliott
Checker	W. Adams
Road Motor Drivers	W. Wonnacott, C. Lidstone, T. Geatches
Night Loco Man	C. Williams

Kingsbridge station staff *c*. 1910 with station master Salmon seated, gold braid, *et al.* In the background a '31XX' class 2-6-2T.
Dermot Reynolds Collection

Kingsbridge goods staff *c*. 1910. The straw hat is worn by the chief clerk.
Dermot Reynolds Collection

Goods guard T. Rich at Gara Bridge *c.* 1912.   *Dermot Reynolds Collection*

Drivers	S. Dunn, R. Canham
Firemen	T. Patrick, (?) Williams
Signalmen	D. Wilson, V. Woolridge

Salcombe Office   A. Hillhouse

Topsham Crossing   H. Stacey

Loddiswell
| Porter in Charge | A. Gidley |
| Permanent Way Gang | G. Garland, H. Reeves, F. Booking, P. Carpenter, H. Fice |

Gara Bridge
| Station Master | K. Cornelius |
| Signalmen | G. Williams, J. Watts |

Occupation Key for permanent way trolley kept in Gara signal box.

Avonwick
| Porter in charge | B. Shelley |

Became unmanned halt from mid-1950s
| Permanent Way Gang | S. Hodge (inspector), W. Hodge, R. Sparks, F. Watts, R. Webber |

Brent
Station Master	P. Bounding
Booking Clerks	Miss J. Jasper
Leading Porter	J. Garland
Porters	M. Roper, I. Bishop, B. Reynolds
Signalmen	G. Hillsom, C. Grove, B. Manning
Shunter	F. Spiller

Goods Office - closed early 1950s
Road Motor provided by Totnes when required.

Station Master

The duties of the station master covered all aspects of operations - the locomotive depot, goods department, signal box and the daily commercial life of the station. He was the 'company' to the local community and his character, honesty, integrity and bearing were essential for good relationships not only with the public but, perhaps more essential, the staff under his control. It was imperative that he kept himself informed of all daily movements, especially goods, to ensure quick turn round of wagons and the smooth and careful handling of goods. There was considerable traffic in livestock for the weekly market (Wednesday) and of course, on his judgement, trucks had to be available to move animals away from the market.

During the course of his duties he was expected to ensure the smooth running of the station, visiting each department daily. He was required to visit the box and inspect the train register book signing his name after the last recorded entry. Another duty was to ensure that copies of the Rule Book were issued to the staff and were kept up to date with all amendments. All monies collected or paid out by the station were his responsibility and to ensure dispatch as detailed further in this chapter.

He was expected by the company to seek new business and also play an active part in local Chamber of Commerce affairs. Kingsbridge being in a holiday area, it was essential that full details of the cheap fares, holiday runabout tickets and luggage in advance facilities were available to the public. Also the company's publication *Holiday Haunts* had to be sold and hoteliers, guest house owners etc., encouraged to take advertising space.

The station master was responsible for ordering and supplying staff coal and collecting and accounting for the monies due. National Savings was popular during the war years and the station master became secretary of the GWR and Western National Staffs' Savings Groups. Having to account for and record transactions of some 50 members was no mean task. The station master had to check all payments claimed for overtime arising from staff shortages and to account for the petty cash disbursements.

In addition to these extra duties, the station master had to be very patient in dealing with all the service organisations, especially when a build up of traffic occurred. There was room for some 120 wagons and at times this figure was exceeded and wagons were held at stations up the branch and even at Brent. As an example of this full capacity, in one weekend 120 wagons of steel runway were received and unloaded by staff for the RAF, the empties being returned to general service. It must be remembered that the local traffic still had to be handled.

Booking and Parcels Office

There were two clerks employed at Kingsbridge full time on booking office duties. Each completed a working week of 42 hours and in order to give cover to all the departing trains their hours were spread as follows:

Early Turn	Late Turn
7.10 am-7.40 am	10.40 am-12.00 noon
9.0 am-1.0 pm	1.0 pm-4.30 pm
2.0 pm-5.0 pm	5.0 pm-7.50 pm

The two clerks changed turns weekly. The early turn clerk took a half day on Saturdays and they changed turns on Wednesdays to enable the late turn clerk to have a half day on that day.

The early turn man was required to 'Book Up' after the departure of each train. He also acted as station cashier, accepting cash from other departments, lorry drivers and the public and at the end of his day prepared a cash remittance statement. The station master then checked the cash and locked this in a leather bag for dispatch next morning by the first train to the district cashier at Plymouth. The early turn clerk was also responsible for ensuring that the travelling safe with the Kingsbridge remittance was placed on the first train each morning. The travelling safe was required to connect at Brent with a stopping service to Plymouth and all stations *en route* were instructed to remit their cash by this means.

The late turn clerk assisted with the above duties during the time the turns overlapped. He was, of course, required to issue tickets and book up the evening trains, also to deal with train enquiries, both counter and telephone, and to list warrants for HM Forces travel etc. In addition he was required to raise charges on 'paid home' parcel deliveries (quite an involved business since a high proportion of the deliveries were outside the 2 miles free limit) and to prepare accounts and send these either direct to the firms concerned or to debit either the sending station or the station handling the firm's account. Charges for forwarded parcels sent on credit were also dealt with in a similar way by this clerk. A variety of parcels statistics were required and this clerk was required to compile this information.

During the course of the evening he telephoned Plymouth station enquiry office with details of the following day's seat reservations for London bound passengers joining the main line train at Brent (except for those travelling by the through coaches on summer Saturdays, which were labelled at Kingsbridge).

There was no overtime payment in those days and the recording for the monthly accounts of the 'next to issue' number of all ticket stock held was a duty taking between one and two hours. Such was the spirit of the staff though, that it was commonplace for the early turn clerk to return at about 7.30 pm to lend a hand to his colleague thereby completing the job more quickly.

As a point of interest the booking off time of 7.50 pm was also the time of departure of the last train giving no time to the clerk for booking up and securing premises.

The monthly proof was the basis of the passenger accounts which, when completed, were sent to the audit office at Aldermaston early each month.

Other duties included the completion of paybills, for the subsequent making up of pay-packets, the stamping of National Insurance cards, maintaining and ordering ticket stock and the requisitioning of stationery.

In addition he provided statistical information of numbers and types of ticket issues for headquarters use. Much of his time was taken in dealing with telephone and counter enquiries as well as with correspondence.

The parcels clerk was also accommodated in the booking office and was responsible for the working of the parcels office dealing with parcels correspondence, quoting rates and charges for parcels sent by passenger train and arranging suitable services for unusual types of traffic particularly where through vehicles were required. He also arranged for the supply of suitable vehicles for the dispatch of fish, livestock, and so on requiring a through vehicle, and the provision of coaches for the through summer Saturday passenger service to Paddington. Details of fish traffic (mainly crabs), perishables and livestock were always wired forward to each transfer point and destination. He also dealt with lost property matters and the parcels department accounts.

The Salcombe receiving office, formerly the premises of Marsh & Co., was principally occupied in dealing with passenger train enquiries, ticket issues, seat reservations and handling Passengers' Luggage in Advance arrangements also taking note of parcels and freight collection orders for the Salcombe lorry driver. The office accepted and charged traffic handed in for dispatch both by passenger and freight service. Payment of traders accounts, particularly for fish traffic and collection of cash for sundry dispatches which had been collected by the Salcombe lorry driver were handled at this office for remittance to Kingsbridge.

The Locomotive Department
There were two drivers, two firemen and a night engineman at Kingsbridge to cover the motive power for the branch. The locomotives were normally '44XX' 2-6-2 tanks ('31XX' before being renumbered) which gave way to the '45XX' and '55XX' locomotives. Newton Abbot was the shed from which the engines were supplied. They were normally changed on Saturdays when it was necessary for two locomotives to be used simultaneously on the branch. The locomotive used during the week would return to Newton late on the Saturday.

The night engineman was booked on at about 11.0 pm to ensure that the engine was ready for the following morning. This engine worked down the branch bunker first so that when it went on shed at the end of the day the smokebox could be emptied into the ash pit. The first job was to clean out the firebox of all ash and clinker and relight the fire under the firebox door. The bunker would then be filled from either the coaling stage or a coal wagon in the bay. (The bunker would hold some three tons of coal.) The engine would still be standing over the pit so the night man would empty the ash pan and clean out the ash from the smoke box around the blast pipe. Whilst doing this job the tubes would be cleared with the steam lance and when the tubes were cleared he could look right down and see the fire glowing in the firebox. Closing the smokebox door he would then spread the fire over the firebox floor and begin to build up a good fire ready for the morning crew. To finish off his duty the night man would clean the engine, back it into the shed and finally clean out the ash pit.

When the engine crew booked on in the morning the fire would be just coming to life. The driver would draw from the stores engine oil (lamps, fire irons, gauge glass lamp etc. would be left on the engine overnight) and drive the engine out of the shed over the pit. It would then be possible to oil the various points requiring lubrication under the engine, at the same time checking springs etc. to make sure no defect would stop the engine. Next he would oil the motion and top up the lubricators on the footplate. Having satisfied himself that all was in order he would then return to the cabin and 'brew up'.

Whilst the driver was performing his duties, the fireman would also be busy. First he would check the fire and make sure steam was being made and see that there was sufficient water in the boiler. Whilst on the footplate he would make sure that the sanding levers were free and operating correctly. Climbing down from the footplate he would then check that the sand boxes were full and, if not, fill them up from the sand bin with dry sand. Moving to the front of the engine he would check that the smokebox was clean and the tubes clear and would then screw up tight the smokebox door to avoid destroying the vacuum in the smokebox when the engine was working, also the possibility of a 'blow back'.

With the night man making up the fire the fireman would then go back onto the footplate and clean the cab, wash down the floor and spray the coal in the bunker to keep down the dust. He would take the engine to the water column and fill the tanks with water. Finally he would ensure that the gauge glass lamp and locomotive lamps were lighted and this done he would join the driver for a 'cuppa'.

With the engine prepared and ready for a day's work, the crew would be ready to start. The signalman by now had booked on and the engine was ready to go off shed and onto the train. The fireman would couple the engine to the train and, during the winter, open the steam heating valve and allow steam to flow into the coach heaters to give a warm welcome to the passengers.

Signal Box

As the signalman came on duty each day he would obtain the key to the box, usually hidden somewhere - and unlock the signal box. The usual procedure was to open the windows in the summer or light the fire in the winter before contacting Gara Bridge signal box, with one beat on the bell - 'Call Attention'. This would be repeated back as acknowledgement, then Kingsbridge would signal: 5 pause-5 pause-5, the code for 'I am opening box', and this also would be acknowledged. When a train was due to depart, the signalman would call attention to Gara and when acknowledged give: 3 pause 1 'are you able to accept branch passenger?'. If Gara Bridge signalman could accept the train he would repeat the code, holding down the plunger after the last stroke thus enabling the Kingsbridge signalman to withdraw the token. All was now clear for the train to enter the single line, so the signalman would lower the signals and pass the token to the driver who could start the train, once the guard had given the 'right away'. The signalman would send 'Train entering section' (2 beats) and would receive 'Train out of section' (2 pause 1) when the train cleared the section to Gara Bridge, complete with tail lamp.

Other duties of the signalman were as follows:

All movement in and out of the station and all bell codes would be recorded in the train register.
Clean and replenish long-burning signal lamps weekly. Check the detonators regularly.
Clean and polish the floor and dust the furniture.
Clean and polish the levers, lamps and all brass work. Black lead the fireplace and lever frame.
Trim the lamps.
Check the box clock against a daily time signal and wind as necessary. Clean all windows, inside and out.
Check batteries in locking room to ensure working correctly. Maintain first aid equipment.

Porters

The porter's job was to assist, wherever possible, in the running of the trains i.e. helping passengers to and from trains, loading and unloading parcels and mail. In addition the station platform, forecourt, offices and toilets had to be cleaned daily, whilst the station notice and advertising boards had to be kept up to date. In later years the station garden blossomed thanks mainly to the efforts of Wally Wilson, the station winning 1st prize in 1960 and 2nd prize in 1961/2/3 - quite an achievement.

Guards

The guard was booked on duty before the first train was scheduled to depart. On arrival at the station he would pick up his bag which contained his flags and detonators, working timetable, a supply of blank train journals and his oil lit hand lamp; in the pockets of his uniform he would of course be carrying a carriage key, whistle and company issued pocket watch.

At Kingsbridge, the coaching stock would be in the platform and was normally made up of one of the two 'B' sets allocated to the branch. Before he could allow the train to depart, the guard would record the coach numbers, check that no unauthorised passengers were aboard (e.g. overnight squatters or tramps); ensure that the communication cord was working properly; check whether the lighting and steam heating equipment was working; ensure the engine was correctly coupled to the coaches (normally the engine was already coupled to the train) and that the hand brakes were released in both brake compartments. Finally he would record the names of the driver and fireman and would advise them of the train load and stops. Hardly necessary for our branch, but it is salutary to reflect that the Great Western's wonderful record was built on the application of firm discipline in small matters so far as its operating staff were concerned.

On returning to his guard's compartment, he would check that the first aid equipment was intact, brake pressure within permitted tolerances and check parcels in luggage compartment to ensure safe handling. There would also be the usual passenger queries to be answered once the train began to fill up. Finally before departure, he would make sure the doors were secure and with a wave of his flag the train would depart. (In the country parts of Devonshire the whistle was probably not used much to 'hurry along' late passengers!)

The Goods Department

This is the department which handled all the larger goods items coming to and from the railway, including livestock. There were three clerks in the office to co-ordinate the flow of traffic and supervise the road vehicle fleet. The traffic handled at Kingsbridge was all the normal goods one associates with a rural area. Wednesday was market day and this brought considerable traffic to the station. Animals arrived early for sale in the market, whilst in the afternoon animals would be moved out.

There were usually three road vehicles based at Kingsbridge, normally

Thornycrofts - and local hauliers were used, as required, to supplement the company vehicles. Freight services were two per day - morning and afternoon, with mixed trains permitted. This was largely reduced to one service per day, towards the end of the branch's life. To handle container traffic and heavy loads, a crane was situated at the end of the yard near to the carriage shed.

As a result of wartime traffic (*see Chapter 5*) and the increase in responsibilities of the station master, Mr Baldwin submitted a request that the station be upgraded to Class 1 status. The content of his application which gives an excellent summary of the work carried out at the station at that time, was as follows:

Dear Sir,

                                            Reclassification
I feel that my additional responsibilities, consequent upon increased wartime traffic, call for a higher salary and I now make application to be raised to Class 1.

Below are some of the developments and changes in the South Hams district which have created an enormous increase in business in the Passenger, Parcels and Goods Departments at this station:

HM Forces
Construction of new stations and installations at various sites and commandeering of many hotels etc., at different places. Present position:

Navy
RNO Salcombe. Naval Depot
HM Naval Establishment, Gara Rock
WRNS Salcombe
Royal Marine Military School, Thurlestone
WRNS Thurlestone

Army
Garrison Engineer, Kingsbridge
RA LAA Kingsbridge
92nd S/L Regt RA Kingsbridge
RAMC 30th Devon's 'C' Coy, Kingsbridge
RTS Kingsbridge
67th LAA Regt Various Batteries. In the fields.
391st Coast Battery RA Salcombe
377 HQVP Coy. CMP Start Point.
30th Bn DCLI 'C' Coy. In the field.
30th Bn DCLI 'D' Coy. Start Point.

Air Force
RAF Air Station, Bolt Head, Soar Aerodrome
RAF Regiment, Bolt Head, Soar Aerodrome
RAF Station, West Prawle
RAF Regiment, West Prawle
RAF Station, Bolt Tail
RAF Station, Hope Cove
RAF Air Sea Rescue Base, Salcombe
RAF Radio location on other sites
WAAF at above stations

Arethusa Training Ship
Shore Establishment, Salcombe.

Civilian Population
In the Kingsbridge urban and rural districts and Salcombe urban district there are large numbers of evacuees and wives and families of members of the forces serving in this area. Some schools and colleges have re-evacuated but the civilian population far exceeds the peace time figure.
The following are additional matters which receive my personal attention and supervision in the passenger and parcels depts:

Moves by Special Trains
Personnel, baggage, stores, ammunition, guns, vehicles of all types, animals etc. Supply and disposal of stock berthings, loading and unloading, formation, etc., also action to ensure 'Moves' being properly booked.

Extra vehicles by Ordinary trains
Deal with all applications received direct from units of HM Forces and the public for conveyance of personnel in large numbers on draft leave or vacations; Horses, Corpses, Stores, Motor Vehicles, Live Stock etc., and arrange the necessary vehicles and train services for the traffic.

Goods Traffic
Since the War, a Special Goods train has run daily, leaving Brent about 10.0 am to convey additional traffic passing to Kingsbridge. Additional traffic also arrives on 'Mixed' trains and 1.50 pm Brent goods.
Outward loaded and empty wagons are cleared by 11.50 am Kingsbridge goods and on 'Mixed' trains or a Special unless Brent is congested and unable to accept.
There is siding accommodation at Kingsbridge for about 78 wagons in position and 42 out of position. During most of the year all the 'in position' room is occupied daily and at frequent periods inwards loaded trucks arrive faster than they can be berthed.
To secure a quick turn round of wagons I give regular supervision at the goods yard, press traders, hauliers, and the Army, Navy or Air Force authorities etc., to special efforts to discharge trucks promptly. Special attention is also given to loads which have to be lifted by crane i.e. drums cable, heavy manhole covers, poles, iron & steel work, agricultural machines of all classes, machinery and electrical apparatus, motor tractors and caravans loaded on trucks without drop sides or ends, large petrol talks, turrets, guns and gun mountings, Whalers and numerous containers. Up to 8 trucks can be berthed ready for the yard crane at one time. These trucks have to be shunted together and then a long shunt has to be made to place them behind about 25 other wagons to get them in position.
Loading bank facilities exist only at the bay line where few trucks can be berthed at one time for sugar beet, scrap iron, broccoli etc. traffic. Here also are dealt with road vehicles of all types from trailer canteens to Bren Gun Carriers which pass over the shoots.
The sidings are dressed by the branch passenger and goods engine as opportunity occurs between arrival and departure of trains, which demands intensive working by all concerned to maintain efficient and economical operation.
The additional traffics consist mainly of:

Inwards
Government traffic of *all* classes including coal and coke for Army, RAF etc.
Government Contractors' traffic of all types for building and maintaining the various stations and installations in this district.
Coal for industrial and household use, manure, grain etc. - waterborne or by road pre-war.
Air raid shelters and hostel equipment.
Wire, tubes etc., for land and water defences.
Containers - increased removals, and bottles for brewery, also for Corona store, and tea for Lyons store.

Outwards
Grain, Barley and Oats for Ministry of Food - increased production; large tonnage.
Scrap iron, waste paper, iron salvage etc. ex-wrecks.
Whalers etc. on special vehicles for Admiralty.
Containers - increased business.
Broccoli - increased production.
Sugar beet - New traffic - 1942/43 season 38 tons.
Bamboo canes - New traffic.
Government stores and ammunition.
Motor cars, caravans and other vehicles on special trucks.
Returned Empties incl. Govt traffic.

Cartage
Our new equipment consists of three 2 ton lorries which operate to capacity as under:
1.   Kingsbridge town goods traffic and as required.
2.   CLS as required and Salcombe goods traffic. Fish ex-Salcombe.
3.   Salcombe lorry.   Non railborne traffic between Kingsbridge and Salcombe. Kingsbridge parcels. Salcombe parcels and as required.
The above equipment is quite inadequate to cope with our cartage work under war time conditions. Assistance has been obtained from other stations for exceptional loads and I have had to hire equipment regularly for work such as:
1.   All Containers 'B' size and over forwarded and received i.e. household removals and bottles to brewery etc.
2.   Collections of rape meal from mills and large tonnage of barley, oats etc., from various farms to station for rail to Ministry of Food.
3.   Deliveries to Kingsbridge and Salcombe of large tonnage cement, also contractors and Government traffic as under to West Prawle, Bolt Head etc: asbestos, asphalt, cable covers, camouflage, cases and cables, GE Co. Cement, coils wire rope, drums cable, concrete slabs, blocks and sections, drums of paint, huts, iron and steelwork, joinery, machinery, mixers, netting, plant, poles, salt for airfield, tanks, tiles, timber, wire mesh etc.
The hauliers have been W.G. Jerwood & Sons whose 5 ton lorries have been very helpful in reducing terminal user time of wagons by quick unloading and loading of heavy consignments. The firm's haulage account has reached £70 per month.

Household Removals
These have been numerous, necessitating personal inspections for estimates in all parts of the district. Charges on outwards removals have varied from £10 to £240 each.
The following are some clerical duties which I have personally undertaken for over two years to ease the pressure in the booking and goods offices where some authorised posts are filled by new entrants:

(1)   Order and regulate supply of staff coal; prepare list of coal required and account for coal sold, bagging & delivery charges, among 55 employees.

(2)   Abstract inwards invoices and balance monthly totals with arrival book; in my own time.

(3)   Hon. Sec. of GWR & Western National Staffs Savings Group; prepare account (Cycle Scheme) and issue NS certificates among 50 members.

(4)   Check overtime sheets. Prepare petty disbursements Summary.

(5)   Wire out forwardings of all livestock & broccoli etc. traffic.

Yours truly,
I. Baldwin

Regrettably for the station master and his staff, this application was rejected by the company. Perhaps if the numbers of passengers and freight tonnage handled had been included, the application may have succeeded. However on the appointment of Mr H. Cox, the station was upgraded to class 1 status, only to revert to class 2 again when Mr C. Talbot was appointed station master, on the retirement of Mr Cox and so it remained until closure.

List of Station Masters at Kingsbridge

9th December, 1893 to 20th March, 1918	F. Salmon
20th March, 1918 to 29th April, 1918	Temporary relief
29th April, 1918 to 17th April, 1920	J. Beard
17th April, 1920 to 20th February, 1931	H.E. Tucker
20th February, 1931 to 1st January, 1941	F. Trewin
1st January, 1941 to 3rd November, 1947	I.C. Baldwin
3rd November, 1947 to 16th December, 1958	H. Cox
16th December, 1958 to 22nd June, 1959	Temporary relief
22nd June, 1959 to 16th September, 1963	C. Talbot

Station closed 16th September, 1963

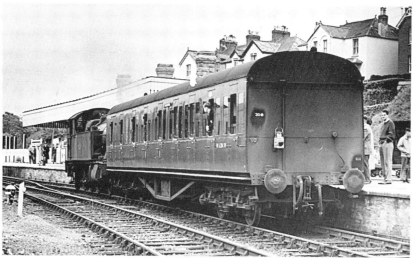

'45XX' Class 2-6-2T No. 4561 arrives at Kingsbridge with the last down steam-hauled service, 10th April, 1961. *Dermot Reynolds Collection*

No. 4561 shunts the stock of the last steam-hauled passenger train at Brent while diesel railcar No. W55017W prepares to leave with its first passenger working to Kingsbridge, 10th April, 1961. *Dermot Reynolds Collection*

The first single unit diesel railcar arrives at Kingsbridge, 10th April, 1961.
Dermot Reynolds Collection

Chapter Eight

The Final Years

Dieselisation of the passenger services came in the spring of 1961 in the form of single unit railcars built by Gloucester Railway, Carriage and Wagon Company, being motor brake seconds - the first to arrive at Kingsbridge being No. W55017. The last regular booked steam freight working was as late as 11th July, 1962.

The diesel units were serviced at Newton Abbot. A through journey was operated during each weekday afternoon to Totnes and the first and last journeys were through workings from and to Newton Abbot respectively as empty stock.

As the summer Saturday timetable included a through working in the morning to Paddington with corresponding arrival during the late afternoon from London of corridor stock - the motive power for these trains over the branch was provided by the North British Type 2, 1,100 hp 'D63XX' class Bo-Bo diesel hydraulic locomotives. These locomotives also hauled the heavier freight trains but steam occasionally appeared on the branch with the normal freight and PW trains.

Rumours of closure were rife as early as the summer of 1962; to the saddened onlooker it seemed as if there was a deliberate policy of running down the branch, particularly as over the previous two years connections had become poor and travellers had longer waits than formerly at Brent.

The background to the future of the line at this time needs to be seen against the problems the British Railways Board faced at this time under its Chairman Dr Richard Beeching. Over the whole of Britain the development of the road system and the increase of both road freight vehicles and private cars was starting to undermine seriously the economic base of the national railway system. Dr Beeching took a major initiative with the support of the Government which aimed at ensuring that money and effort was directed to those parts of the system which everyone was certain had a long term future and had reasonable hopes of making a profit - or at least of not losing money.

Thus branch lines - and the Kingsbridge line was one of many - had to justify their future in terms of their branch revenue and costs. The evaluation system used seemed very harsh to those who saw their local lines as valuable feeders to the main lines; the unpalatable truth was that the main line portion of through revenue was needed to balance the books on the main lines themselves, together with the fact that seasonal summer Saturday traffic itself tended to be uneconomic to cater for in the financial circumstances of the post-war years - the coaches required having to stand idle for most of the year.

Thus at this time the British Railways Board had no incentive to try and save a line; it did not deliberately run down; rather the converse, it did not deliberately build up or rehabilitate, because it had other priorities, which were firmly supported by the Government of the day.

But of course this was not how local people saw pending events. The local

'55XXX' railcar leaves Loddiswell with an up train in June 1961. *Lens of Sutton*

A diesel railcar enters Kingsbridge station with the 6.40 pm from Brent in the Summer of 1962.
Dermot Reynolds Collection

council was naturally conscious of the importance of the railway, as an element in local transport. Thus the battle to keep the line open began; formal notices of the intended closure were posted at all stations on the branch on 27th March, 1962, thus confirming that the threat of closure was now very real.

On hearing of the threat of closure, the local branch of ASLEF printed and distributed leaflets headed 'No Railway for Kingsbridge' calling for a public protest, adding that the closure would mean the death of the South Hams. The local Chamber of Trade said that they had anticipated closure and were very unhappy at losing the railway, a view also held by the local councils. This leaflet culminated in a public meeting on 29th June, 1962 attended by 120 people. The resolve of this meeting was to organise a petition against closure and to seek the support of the local authorities.

The petition read as follows:

We, the undersigned, being residents of the South Hams area ask the BTC to hold any move to close the Kingsbridge branch line until there has been a full public enquiry into the circumstances.

A further proposal by Mr B. Stone was also adopted, reading as follows:

We hereby petition the Ministry of Transport that rather than close the Kingsbridge branch line, to take steps to increase the passenger service, improve the efficiency of the service and make additional effort to make the railway service economic.

Despite the enthusiasm at the meeting, subsequently some hostility was aroused, some people saying that it was all a political plot by being held under the auspices of ASLEF and the Kingsbridge Labour Party. The chair was taken by Mr R. Bryant, Chairman of ASLEF Newton Abbot, Secretary was Mr L. Lamb, (Secretary of ASLEF Newton Abbot) and the principal speaker Mr R. Scott, prospective Labour candidate for Totnes division. However, this meeting did crystallise public opinion although perhaps there were some political overtones.

Following this meeting a joint meeting of the local councils was held on 4th July, 1962 and this august body resolved to support the public petition feeling that they also had the support of the railwaymen. They further resolved to write a letter of protest to their member of Parliament, Mr R. Mawby, and to seek his support in placing their case before the Minister.

The Chamber of Trade met that same evening and pledged its support for the petition and suggested the setting up of a preservation society, on the lines of the Bluebell Railway. A letter was also to be sent to Mr F.G. Dean, Plymouth district traffic superintendent, reminding him of the promise made in 1957, by him, to keep the Chamber advised of any changes concerning the railway. However, at that time there were no firm proposals for Mr Dean to comment upon.

The first opportunity the local authorities and residents had to air their grievances formally was at the public enquiry on 26th November, 1962 held by the South West Transport Users' Consultative Committee, which had the duty of reporting to the Ministry of Transport.

Table 92 BRENT and KINGSBRIDGE (for Salcombe)

WEEK DAYS ONLY (Second class only)

Miles		am		am	noon		pm		pm		pm						
	Brent .. .. .. dep	7 20	..	9 45	..	12 0	..	1 25	..	5 22	..	6 40	..	..	..	..	..	..
2¼	Avonwick	7 26		9 51		12 6		1 31		5 28		6 46						
5¼	Gara Bridge	7 33		9 58		1213		1 38		5 35		6 53						
9	Loddiswell Halt	7 41		10 6		1221		1 46		5 43		7 1						
12¼	Kingsbridge .. .. arr	7 50		1015		1230		1 55		5 52		7 10						
—	Salcombe ¶ ...... arr	8 25		1058		1 28		2 28		6 33		8 3						

Miles		am B		am		am		pm B		pm		pm A						
—	Salcombe ¶ .. dep	6 55	..	9 30	..	1130	..	1 30	..	4C30	..	5G35	..	..	..	..	..	..
—	Kingsbridge .... dep	8 0		1025		1235		2 5		5 58		7 20						
3¼	Loddiswell Halt ..	8 10		1035		1245		2 15		6 8		7 30						
7	Gara Bridge	8 16		1041		1251		2 21		6 14		7 36						
10	Avonwick	8 23		1048		1258		2 28		6 21		7 43						
12¼	Brent .... arr	8 30		1055		1 5		2 35		6 28		7 50						

A To Newton Abbot (Table 81)
B To Totnes (Table 81)

C Commencing 3rd June, 1963 dep
   5 0 pm
G Commencing 3rd June, 1963 dep
   6 0 pm

¶ By Western National Omnibus
(Heavy luggage not conveyed)

Road Services are also operated from Kingsbridge to Thurlestone and Hope

Timetable for Summer 1963.

A '55XXX' railcar at Gara Bridge with 12.00 pm from Brent, on 19th July, 1963.

Dermot Reynolds Collection

Devon County Council objected to piecemeal closure of branch lines and hoped that any decision on this branch closing would be deferred until the Government had reviewed its overall railway plan in 1963, taking the view that once the line is closed, it would be more difficult to reopen. BR had stated that Totnes would be the railhead for the South Hams and the Western National Omnibus would run in the region of six through services daily to Salcombe via Kingsbridge from Totnes with BR hiring the buses for exclusive use of rail passengers.

Despite requests for relevant financial figures, BR had still not furnished a breakdown of the costs of operating the line. However, at the public enquiry, BR, presented certain costs for the branch which, summarised, were as follows:

Wage Bill	£22,408	Revenue for branch	£16,022
Repair of stock	3,382		
Fuel, water etc.	3,231		
Day to day maintenance			
(P. Way/Buildings)	3,030		
Provision for renewals	908	Therefore expected loss	
Provision for track renewals	4,800	per annum	21,737
	£37,579		£37,759

There were some discrepancies. Why the provision of wages for two passenger and three goods guards? Surely it was unfair to charge the whole of these wages to the branch. Similarly, four drivers wages should surely be only three. Therefore, in our opinion, by reducing this wage bill to two guards and three drivers, a saving of £1,300 pa could have been made.

The passenger revenue only included that booked on the branch, but excluded Brent. The figures for 1960 of £12,825, and 1961 (est.) £13,600, suddenly drop to an estimate of £9,047 in 1964 which seems unlikely. The recasting of the timetable must have contributed to the loss of passengers. There was a departure from Kingsbridge at 8.0 am with an arrival in Plymouth at 9.57 am - a wait at Brent of 45 mins. Previously, the train left at 7.35 am with an arrival in Plymouth at 8.45 am. Surely this drove passengers to other forms of transport.

Despite the economies, it still left a loss of around £21,000 pa. But undoubtedly other economies could have been made with some staff savings - preferable to wholesale closure. An improvement in connections at Brent and the possible use of steam as a tourist attraction (e.g. like the Vale of Rheidol in central Wales) would, we feel sure, have brought a substantial increase in passenger revenue.

Reverting back to revenue, how many Runabout tickets bought off the branch were never apportioned to the branch? The through bookings on Saturdays must be another example.

In our researches at the archives of the Record Office at BR, documents showing the branch traffic on an annual basis for the years 1935-1958 inclusive, were located. It is interesting to compare these figures with those used in the Inquiry by the Board:

	1957	1958	1959	1960	1961	1964
Passengers booked	22,389	20,783	16,293	13,875	13,350	n/a
Revenue	£15,174	£13,795	£12,140	£12,825	£13,260	£9,047
Parcel Revenue	£6,935	£6,014	n/a	n/a	n/a	£707
Goods tonnage handled	12,722	12,677	n/a	n/a	n/a	n/a

As can be seen, the passenger traffic dropped quite considerably between 1957 and 1960, but by 1961 seemed to be levelling off. It has not been possible to obtain figures for 1962 or 1963 and the 1964 figure is the estimate of traffic the Board considered would be lost with closure. The revenue discrepancy for passengers is quite amazing. Fare increases should have maintained the existing revenue, despite the drop in passengers.

The parcels revenue is also quite drastically reduced from 1957/8 to BR's estimate of 1964. One wonders how a trade of £6,000 pa reduces to £700 in 6 years. Again during the intervening years there were increases in carriage charges and new business could have been canvassed.

In retrospect and reviewing the distressing figures of a reducing rail traffic, one realises how relentless at this period was the onward march of the road vehicle (particularly the motor car), encouraged as it was by road modernisation and motor fuels at prices which no one found particularly exorbitant.

The goods traffic was not disclosed at the Inquiry, there was a healthy tonnage handled on the branch and much of this traffic was lost, for good, to the road haulage industry. It was estimated by the staff that the tonnage in 1962 was in excess of 12,000 tons, but in 1963 the branch was poorly patronised, as local organisations made alternative arrangements.

The local coal merchant - John Westcott Ltd - in Kingsbridge took delivery of approximately 3,000 tons of coal each year by rail. With the closure, this traffic would be handled at Totnes and then by road vehicle to Westcott's Yard. It was estimated that this additional road journey would cost in the region of 10 shillings per ton and reimbursement was obtained from BR by way of compensation.

Objections to the closure were raised by Salcombe and Kingsbridge Councils, stating that present bus services were very poor and travel within the area would be most difficult. It was also feared that there would be a drop in visitors causing financial loss to the local traders, hoteliers and catering organisations. The County Secretary of the NFU stated that his members were worried regarding the speedy, efficient and prompt delivery of broccoli, flowers and especially strawberries and soft fruit. In addition, there was concern over the transit of one day old chicks and the annual sugar beet crop. It was claimed that 1,500 tons of beet were handled annually at the station. Further objections from local traders were made by the Chelford Yacht and Launch Company who complained of the double handling of expensive yachts and boats with possibility of damage.

Local residents complained of hardship, especially Mrs Mavis Lavender, a mother of eight children, from Gara Bridge. Mrs Lavender stated that there was no alternative means of transport for people living at Gara Bridge and that should the line close, she would have to move. Subsequently, she eventually moved to Totnes. A Mrs Phillimore stated that she regularly used the line and had written direct to the Minister (Mr Marples).

With the severe winter at the beginning of January 1963, the railway came into its own again. The roads were blocked but the railway continued to function. Driver Canham and guard Jerred, both of Kingsbridge, were a welcome sight to the isolated farmers of the South Hams.

A train loaded with essential supplies departed from Kingsbridge calling at all stations, also at Topsham Bridge and Bickham Bridge. Groceries, bread, animal foodstuffs and fuel were left along the line for redistribution by tractors and sledges.

During this period, the line was exceptionally busy with passengers endeavouring to get to business etc., it being estimated that over 1,000 people travelled at this time. Despite the snow the trains got through.

It was indeed fortunate for the Lavender family that the trains were running. Living at Gara Bridge, they were completely cut off, and on one occasion Mrs Lavender needed hospital treatment. Fortunately, as the trains were running, Mr Lavender was able regularly to visit his wife in hospital in Plymouth.

As late as 2nd September, 1963, the council were still hopeful of a reprieve, blaming civil servants for the closure of rural railway services. Heated arguments broke out in the council's finance and general purposes committee and order was eventually restored by Councillor E. Hamer. The committee, however, again raised serious doubts about the promised replacement bus services.

The last day of full steam operated passenger trains was Saturday 10th April, 1961, but a diesel railcar set in fact worked the last down passenger on the Saturday evening (8.45 pm ex-Brent). However, due to late running of the Penzance-Manchester train which connected with the branch train, departure was delayed until 9.15 pm. On busy Saturdays, steam ran extra services.

The last booked up steam working, hauled by No. 4561, was the 7.30 pm service from Kingsbridge and to make this last steam run, members of the Kingsbridge Model Engineering Club travelled to Brent and back. At this time BR estimated that for every £100 taken in income on the branch, it cost £350 to maintain and operate the branch. Driver Canham drove both of these trains.

During the last week of operations on the branch, Mr C.H. Blythe of Thurlestone chartered a special restaurant car train to take dinner on the branch as a farewell to the railway. The fare for the trip and dinner was £2 10s. inclusive. On 10th September, 1963, the party of 79 travelled from Kingsbridge on the 5.45 pm dmu to Brent where they detrained to join the special. The special train of four coaches was headed by No. 4555, the last steam locomotive to work the branch. The crew were provided by Laira shed being driver W. Hood and fireman A. Jones. The whole set including the kitchen car had worked down the same day in the 'Cornishman' (Sheffield-Plymouth).

The special was scheduled to depart from Brent at 6.55 pm stopping at Gara Bridge for dinner to be served. Leaving at 8.00 pm the special was due to arrive at Kingsbridge at 8.20 pm. After running round, the train was scheduled to leave at 8.30 pm to Brent and then empty stock to Laira. At least that is what should have happened.

However things soon began to hum as reminiscence and 'refreshment' combined to give the occasion that well known feeling that time is not all

A railcar about to leave Kingsbridge just prior to the line's closure.   *Dermot Reynolds Collection*

Crowds gather to watch the last passenger train working from Kingsbridge, 14th September, 1963.   *Dermot Reynolds Collection*

important; the schedule was soon forgotten.

The catering arrangements were made by the Restaurant Car Manager at Plymouth. However, although the original allocation of drink was doubled, the supply soon became exhausted.

The train proceeded down the branch where it went remarkably slowly at times, as all the past employees on the line had been told to be around, and there was considerable passing out of the train of various bottles (all full) which were being drunk with gay abandon. Eventually the train arrived at Avonwick which took only 10 to 15 minutes. The train was out of whisky so the Restaurant Car Manager, who was acting as the *Maitre d'Hotel* on the train went off with the conductor to negotiate for another two cases at the local pub. Shades of the ceremony in January 1891 when the first sod was cut.

Subsequently the passengers had a sweep - the winner to pull the communication cord. The officials naturally could not agree to this, but of course if it happened they would have to go through the usual safety procedure. By some strange coincidence, the communication cord was pulled and the train stopped on Topsham level crossing. One of the passengers detrained with a glass for the crossing keeper whilst the guard went forward following his normal course of safety duties. A motorist who was in a new car, was so surprised at a train being stopped - and a steam driven train at that - that he got out of his car leaving the engine running and the door open. He leant over the gate to ask a number of passengers what was going on, and was invited on board for a 'noggin'. Just as he got into the train the crossing party reboarded, and the train left. His car was still standing in the road with the door open and the engine running! He was able to return about three hours later.

And so it went on; from a very late dinner at Kingsbridge, to an even later departure for Brent. Constant blowing of the whistle on the way back to Brent brought complaints from farmers about cattle being frightened which resulted in calls from the Police to Control at Plymouth. The Passenger Manager eventually had to go into the signal box at Brent and do a 'smoothing down' operation with Divisional Control, the Police and everybody else. The Control log records the 'Special' back at Plymouth at 12.40 am.

The Minister acted swiftly; complete closure and lifting of the track - with Kingsbridge goods depot alone to remain as a road facility served from Totnes - was approved and the date fixed for the last weekday of the summer service - 7th September, 1963. Yet as late as 31st August that year the 9.10 am through train to Paddington with a 'D63XX' at the head of a four-coach train with some 200 people aboard was seen to pull out of Kingsbridge. Incredible indeed that a line which could support such a service was wiped off the map.

Closure was, in fact, postponed for a week to enable the Western National Omnibus Company to obtain the necessary authority from the Traffic Commissioners for their new through service from Salcombe to Totnes and for other additional services required by the Minister. These really only amounted to no more than one daily service to and from Loddiswell station and one to California Cross.

It was a busy day at the station on 14th September, still being in the holiday season. The last through train of four coaches departed at 11.00 am, being well filled with passengers for Paddington - station master Talbot's last major train. Enthusiasts mingled with locals during the day and great lengths of film were expended in recording the sad events of a closure.

The last down train arrived, composed of a 2-car dmu and the branch single car, adorned with a wreath but the coaches were not clean. As the full load of passengers de-trained a Scandinavian film crew also recorded the scene.

Despite the sad occasion some 160 people turned out to travel on the last passenger train. The civic party was led by the Chairman of Kingsbridge Urban District Council (Coun. W.J. Lewis), together with representatives of Kingsbridge Rural District Council. Two notable travellers were Messrs Stidston and Nunn who had travelled on the first day in December 1893. The train was scheduled to depart at 5.33 pm - the normal service time - and in true GWR fashion attached to the rear of the train was a fish van containing two tons of fresh fish.

At Gara Bridge Mrs Mavis Lavender - who figured prominently at the Public Inquiry over the closure of the line - accompanied by her daughter Pamela, aged 10 years, met the train for the last time. Soon it would be time to leave, with whistles blowing, guard Tanner waved his flag and driver Grubber slowly drew over the level crossing and accelerated away from the station. The train rumbled off into the gathering gloom heading for Avonwick and Brent.

Memories were stirred for a Mr Huxham, who saw operations on the first day of services (1893), when he viewed the last day. Mr Huxham said that on the first day everywhere was bright and gay, whilst the train was gleaming with brasswork shining, and carriages in the well known GWR colours.

Wally Wilson with the last train, complete with wreath, 14th September, 1963.

Dermot Reynolds

I stood in a field near the cutting at Sorley and waited for the last train. Into view came a dark and shabby diesel train, looking very dirty. What a sad contrast to the elegant train of the GWR 70 years before.

In the meantime Mr T.W.E. Roche was actively engaged in obtaining the support of the Joint Railway Committee of both Kingsbridge and Salcombe UDC's to take over and run the branch privately, as had been done on the Bluebell line. The branch was given the title of 'The Primrose Line' which really fitted the picture very well - the branch was to be kept open in the winter as a social service, and run as a tourist attraction in the summer.

Offers of support to the scheme came from many quarters. The then infant Great Western Society had just purchased a '14XX' tank No. 1466 and was looking for a branch on which to operate; success surely was just around the corner.

Mr Roche wrote to the divisional manager in Plymouth on 11th October outlining their proposals and requesting a figure for the purchase of the line and equipment - the manager at the time being Mr F.D. Pattisson, while Mr G.F. Fiennes had just taken over as General Manager at Paddington.

Administrative confusion at Paddington prevailed in spite of the courtesy and co-operation shown by these two most able gentlemen.

At that time the British Railways Board attached great importance to the quick realisation of scrap, so that capital for financing the further modernisation of the system could be found from this source. Thus the Contracts Department at Paddington, in fulfilling the Board's directive to move more quickly, were actually signing lifting contracts with a firm of scrap metal merchants whilst Mr Roche was still engaged in his negotiations to save the line. He met the three local councils in Kingsbridge in November 1963 at which time they gave their undertaking to take over the line, but there was still some uncertainty about the future of Brent and of course, the imminent lifting. As T.W.E. Roche walked out of the council chamber up to the station yard, he walked straight into the arms of the first of the contractor's men, armed with oxyacetylene lamps, compressors, wrenches and so on, and had the unhappy privilege of witnessing the first rivet on the branch being undone.

The project was, therefore, regretfully abandoned, the many supporters who had donated to the 'Primrose Railway Preservation Fund' were urged to transfer their support to the Dart Valley Line - happily, this project lives to portray for generations to come that magical beauty of the Devonshire branch line.

Track lifting began in November 1963 and was completed by May 1964. The contractor was Geo. Cohen, and the track is reputed to have been sold to an Eastern European country for re-use. As the branch was re-laid in 1961 (!) it had many years of useful life left.

It was stated at the time by T.W.E. Roche that the price asked by the Board for the line complete, including the land, was £24,000. There was some doubt as to whether this included access to the bay at Brent, but it was assumed that it did. The funds readily available were approximately £20,000 and it was hoped that local authorities would raise the balance, and with the co-operation of the Great Western Society, the stock would be found to operate the line. However, the scrap contract had been signed allegedly for £18,000 - and that was the end of any preservation schemes.

Driver Ron Canham and his fireman at Brent.   *Dermot Reynolds*

Driver Ron Canham (*left*) fills No. 4561's tank in readiness for the last up steam-hauled service
from Kingsbridge, 10th April, 1961.   *Dermot Reynolds*

Chapter Nine

Characters and Reminiscences

Naturally over the years a country branch, such as the Kingsbridge, created its very own special characters, many of whom are long since forgotten. But thankfully many remain, without whose assistance, this book would have been incomplete.

Whole families were connected with 'The Western' and for such a small but very dedicated band of local folk - it was their life.

It was a friendly line - in the early years one driver, Bob Hine, fixed his engine whistle and this would emit his own particular signal so that when passing his village of Loddiswell, his family would be aware he would soon be home.

Naturally, with the line running for such a distance alongside the River Avon - a notable salmon river - many a fishing tale can be told. It was once said that the construction navvies destroyed the salmon with explosives as a relaxation from the blasting of Sorley tunnel. 'T'was nevar ben tha same mi dears.' Many 'up country' folk came for the sport. Bailiffs employed by the landowners patrolled their respective beats and poaching was rife and very lucrative. It was not long before the enterprising poacher 'chatted up' the engine crews, asking them to notify him where the bailiff was patrolling by an advance warning system. This worked well, a whistle system was perfected - the crew were suitably rewarded - all were happy.

The branch had a very good safety record, but one of the earliest recalled accidents appears to have concerned a freight train on the main line jumping the facing points on the down line at Brent and blocking the branch line, not very serious but causing annoying delays. Another occurred in the late 1940s when a ganger was killed by a locomotive outside Loddiswell station whilst walking on the track - the Kingsbridge driver was not aware of the incident until the local police called at his house in the early morning advising him the ganger's cap had been found on the buffer beam of his locomotive.

There are numerous tales of loose animals straying onto the line; but on one occasion on an evening up train the Kingsbridge engine crew, Messrs Aldridge and Dunn, noticed some object ahead just outside Avonwick. Cautiously the brakes were applied just as the outline of a young stallion appeared. Gingerly they crept forward but so did the stallion - this went on for a mile or more and as the main line was approaching a disastrous fate could befall the poor creature should it stray in front of an oncoming express. Fortunately, the GWR emergency whistle in conjunction with the normal whistle, frightened the poor beast away into the night, yards short of the main line.

There is many a tale that can be told of the experiences of travellers during World War II. As we have previously related, the South Hams played a major part in the training of Allied forces on the projected Normandy landings. An entire area was evacuated, whole families were moved to relatives out of the area which was bounded by Strete, Slapton, Chillington and Blackawton.

Kingsbridge fortunately suffered very little from enemy attack, but one dark rainy winter's evening, the 7.45 pm for Brent was about to leave when a German Heinkel swooped low over the town and sighting the glow of the firebox in the evening dark, decided this must be an important railhead which should be destroyed. Unaware they had been spotted, the crew set off for Brent; approaching Rake Cutting, driver Dunn heard the unfamiliar scream of an aircraft and there could be no mistake that they were the target. Sorley tunnel was only about 500 yards away - with one almighty jerk the regulator was slammed wide open. Fortunately the fireman had a full head of steam and the little 'prairie' nearly took off. As driver Dunn recalled in later years, that 500 yards seemed more like 500 miles although it was surely the fastest ascent of Sorley Bank ever. Just as the train entered the tunnel, a smothered thud of an explosion could be heard - but they were clear - the bombs had landed on the top of the tunnel, all were safe. A cautious exit from the northern end revealed their attacker had made for home.

Blackout was rigidly enforced in the country during World War II, as it was in the cities. A certain weary traveller enquired of the guard before the departure of the 9.40 pm from Brent how he would know when the train had reached his station - Loddiswell - as all would be in darkness. The confident guard replied 'Mi dear 'tis simple. See this platform. You gets orf on this side. You counts th' stops and yous gets orf at th' third stop. Alright mi dear, 'tis simple.' The traveller agreed, and no doubt was taken by the quaint and delightful charm of the Devon accent. Just as the train was leaving the off duty crossing keeper from Topsham Bridge who had hitched a lift on the up 7.45 pm from Kingsbridge for a few quick jars in Brent - came running down the platform from the direction of the road bridge, then climbed on the footplate of the '45XX'; off they set. Our traveller, sitting in his seat, was patiently counting the stops. At the second, he clearly heard the station master - probably Bill Hough - call out 'Geara Bridge, Geara Bridge' - a familiar cry to the regular traveller. He then prepared himself to 'exit left' at the next stop. The train pulled up, he heard voices, and knew this was the third stop. Opening the door, luggage in each hand, he stepped for the - nothing!! Fortunately it had been raining, his landing was soft on the river bank and the crossing keeper came running back, having just alighted, to open the Topsham Bridge crossing gates. One can imagine our weary town traveller with suit and patent leather shoes covered in red Devon soil. The keeper cried out, 'What 'e doin 'ere mi dear?' His reply we leave to your imagination.

One of the station staff - Mr F.E. Drew - joined the RAF and was subsequently promoted to flying officer. In 1943 he was awarded the Distinguished Flying Cross and the *GWR Magazine* carried a short paragraph as follows:

Flying Officer F.E. Drew, of the Royal Air Force, has been awarded the Distinguished Flying Cross in recognition of great navigational ability displayed throughout his many operational sorties against targets in enemy country and on mine laying expeditions. He has recently made successful long distance flights and has participated in a daylight attack over Italy. This officer has displayed remarkable calmness under the most trying circumstances and his consistent success is described as worthy of the highest praise. Prior to joining the Forces, Flying Officer Drew was a clerk at Kingsbridge station.

In 1944, now Flight Lieutenant Drew, he was shot down over enemy territory. The *GWR Magazine* has a briefer note saying that Flight Lieutenant Drew was reported as being a prisoner of war in Germany.

Regrettably, efforts to trace Mr Drew in later years have proved hopeless. He did not return to Kingsbridge after the war was over but we hope he survived and may possibly read this book.

Routine operation of a branch became almost automatic to the many drivers on the line and it was on one such occasion that a driver became so preoccupied in discussion with the Brent signalman that he forgot to take the token - eased off the brakes, and opened the regulator. Just as he reached the end of the platform, having taken for granted the branch starter was off, he saw the Divisional Engineer's inspection train emerging from the branch! On another occasion, the driver of a down train approaching Topsham crossing was puzzled to see the distant signal on, applied the brakes just north of the crossing, to find the keeper struggling to free half a dozen hounds trapped under the gate!

The engine crews were mainly Kingsbridge men. Joe Higgins spent most of his driving life on the branch from 1904 until he retired, as did driver Dunn Senior. The crews mainly stayed together as they became accustomed to one another's methods of working. Ron Canham and Ray Burgess were firm favourites, especially with 'us' young lads - having the occasional run on the footplate round the run-round loop. Ron Canham had the distinction of driving the last steam passenger train out of Kingsbridge and the first diesel unit into Kingsbridge. Actually the latter occasion was not without its drama. Ron Canham duly took the controls of the gleaming green Gloucester RC&W Co. single unit - No. W55017 - but nothing on this earth could persuade this fiendish new device to draw away. All the right buttons were pressed, the main control opened - no go. It was not before checking the unit from end to end that Ron found the brake release handle in his pocket - then they were off. Another occasion involving a diesel unit running through to Newton Abbot to connect with the up 'Torbay Express', found there were so many people in the car that the doors fouled the platform - regrettably not a common occurrence.

There was great uproar on one occasion when cattle were being loaded. A bullock decided to take some exercise and leapt out over the pen. Heading up behind the goods shed, the signalman chased the animal off only for it to go up the bank behind the box towards the shed. Leaping down from behind the shed the beast shot round by the end of the station building, between the bay and the platform. Seeing the end of the platform coming up, he sat down and skidded over the edge of the rails. However, a would-be passenger, thought to be the owner of the bullock, tried to stop the beast and promptly got gored by the horns and needed first aid. The bullock turned and rumbled off down towards the carriage shed where the carriage cleaner was at work. Spying the animal charging towards him, he used a bucket of cold dirty water at the appropriate moment and turned the animal away. Trapped by the gate, the bullock surrendered and was duly shipped out of Kingsbridge.

The GWR Salcombe office came under the authority of the station master at Kingsbridge. One summer afternoon a lady called in at the Salcombe office for train information.   After much discussion, it was established that several changes of train were required and the details were given to the lady. Shortly after her departure, the office closed for the day. The clerk (Eric Gillard) caught the bus to Kingsbridge to pay his day's takings in at Kingsbridge and at the same time assist his colleague who was very busy with all the holiday traffic. Eric answered a call at the enquiry office to meet face to face the Salcombe lady asking the same travel query. The answer: the train times given at Salcombe were the same used at Kingsbridge and the lady left reassured.

There is a story of a late arrival for duty by one of the station staff. Apparently a thick fog had come down. Riding his motor cycle he was taking great care when suddenly an elephant appeared in the middle of the road. Braking sharply, he skidded and took a dive over the hedge. Fortunately, he was not too badly hurt and was able to continue on to work. The elephant was loose from the local circus.

Before World War II the circus special was a regular event on the branch - bringing unusual vehicles - 'Monster' road/rail trucks, 'Siphons' etc. - to Kingsbridge. Post war, this train ran less and less and finally ceased in the mid-1950s.

The arrival of this train brought the keen gardeners of the staff 'hot foot' when cleaning out operations began. On one occasion the staff carefully opened the end doors of a 'Monster', positioned at the bay, to let the elephants out and were confronted in the darkness by a little man, dark skinned, and smelling strongly of his charges. It is believed he was English and not of Eastern origin. When the animals had left, the vehicles were shunted to the cattle dock for cleaning, washing and disinfecting. Elephants are large, lumbering, heavy and slow moving animals, but they have been known not to enter vehicles unless they are spotlessly clean; and if an elephant does not want to move, there is no way of persuading it. It is at this point that trouble began. As the dung was thrown out, eager gardeners stockpiled the highly smelling dung for use in the garden. When operations were complete there were three large piles of manure on the ground. How to mark which was which? Our three intrepid gardeners were loathe to leave in case one of the others should steal his pile. In the end compromise was reached when three labels were nailed to a wooden stake, with names on, and stuck in the appropriate pile.

There is another tale concerning the loading of a wagon for dispatch; some goods were being labelled. A keen porter was making out the wagon labels and quickly putting them in the wagon clips.   In the haste another employee shouted out 'old em', to be interpreted as Oldham on the label.   Yes, you guessed right, the wagon was consigned to Oldham, Lancs.

A respected citizen of Kingsbridge was a regular traveller on the railway and made many long distance journeys. The station staff quite enjoyed booking this gentleman, as he insisted on buying his tickets in the bar of the Crabshell Inn and there was always a pint of beer for the staff during the transaction.

Wally Wilson, after rejoining the railway in the 1950s from being seconded to Western National in 1929, took a keen interest in the station garden and soon had flowers and shrubs growing in the neat beds on the platform.

On summer Saturdays, towards the end of steam, the train crews used to play tricks on their unsuspecting colleagues. Gara Bridge was the passing place and the up train crew would stop in the platform with the engine hose pipe at the ready. When the down train ran in over the level crossing, they would spray the cab with water and soak the unlucky occupants. A variation crept in on one occasion. The up train arrived and the driver, complete with bucket of water, got down and walked to the rear of the train. The down train crew ran in and were seen hunched up in the corner of the cab awaiting a soaking. Nothing happened. A relieved driver stopped his train and smiling, looked out of his cab only to receive a bucket of water right in his face. Caught again!

As has been related elsewhere in the book, the winters could be very cold especially at Gara Bridge where there was no gas, no electricity, no mains sewage and no running water. With so many trees around, it is not surprising that they would end up in the fireplace.

On several occasions the ganger's trolley was used to assist in various schemes. On one occasion, several trees had to be felled near Topsham. The trees were duly felled, but how to get them to Gara? - the pump trolley. The trolley was run up to the spot and loaded on board and back to Gara. A similar use was made of the trolley in moving a piano from Gara to Loddiswell.

During the winter of 1958 a serious storm developed with heavy rain and gale force winds. The trees were bending under the force and the Gara station master realised that something might happen to disrupt services. The last down train (9.20 pm ex-Brent) was running about 30 mins late and he heard it pass on towards Kingsbridge. About 25 mins later there was a knock on his door and it was the signalman (Gordon Williams) to say that the train had hit a tree which had been blown down. Donning gum boots and sou-wester the station master went to the station. On his arrival he was told that the electric train staff equipment was defective. Summoning the lineman, Vic Poole from Brent, the party set off with suitable tools and Tilley lamps. Driver Dunn had reported no damage to the engine.

On their arrival at the scene of the fallen tree it was soon noticed that the signal and telephone wires were bowed down by a large tree. By the light of the Tilley lamps, the party began to cut up the tree. The tree had fallen across the line and was held up by the wires which surprisingly had not broken. Eventually they cut back the tree to the wires and were faced with the problem of how to move the tree without breaking them. By grouping the wires altogether, a swift, accurate blow with a steel bar and the tree dropped to the ground and with a tremendous and deafening crack all the wires sprang back into position. Tidying up and clearing all obstructions, the party set off back to Gara, tired and cold, but again due to the experience of professional railwaymen, a tricky problem was solved. At midnight they were able to test the equipment in the box and the Kingsbridge signalman - Jan Cazely - reported that the token equipment was working correctly. No delays were experienced by travellers the following morning and very few people knew of the efforts made during the night.

In about 1905 a Mr Pulleyblank planted a pure white rose tree in the garden on the up side, by the signal box at Gara Bridge. This rose flowered twice a year and gave considerable pleasure to all those using the station. In 1957, the signal department lopped the tree so that the box could be painted. However, the rose objected to this harsh treatment and it took two years of loving care and attention before it would finally bloom again.

The first flowers to bloom as winter drew to its close at Gara were snowdrops. Despite the snow on the ground, the snowdrops raised their heads to the world and were a real picture.

View looking out of the north portal of Sorley tunnel, July 1994.   *Dermot Reynolds*

Chapter Ten

Epilogue

Since writing the epilogue to the first edition 20 years have passed and the unrelenting march of man and nature have further erased traces of the line's existence - houses have been built on part of the trackbed in Kingsbridge, the northern embankment leading into Sorley tunnel has been removed, and the A38 Exeter to Plymouth trunk road has almost completely obliterated any trace of the branch either side - these are just a few of the developments.

Most of the small structures on the branch were destroyed by the scrap contractors and later by souvenir hunters. The Kingsbridge and Gara Bridge signal boxes were completely destroyed - the once gleaming levers, frame and locking devices, lay a tangled heap of scrap metal. The late T.W.E. Roche refers to a photograph in his book *Go Great Western* taken by Bryan Gibson named 'Despair' outside the partially dismantled Kingsbridge signal box.

The station nameboards together with all the station furniture were removed shortly after closure and loaded on the last up goods train.

The Kingsbridge station site is now a thriving industrial estate, the main station building remain largely intact with extensions and the canopy now completely enclosed. The magnificent goods shed also remains intact.

Most of the iron bridges were removed by the contractors with one notable exception - the three-road bridge just south of Gara Bridge station. Many of the stone road and river bridges remain, one majestic twin arch bridge spanning the River Avon just north of Loddiswell station will remain for many years to come.

All the stations are now private residences, Loddiswell has been particularly well restored complete with station nameboard, milk churns, and period signs. At the time of writing cream teas are served under the canopy during the summer season.

The crossing keeper's cottage at Topsham Bridge is also a private residence albeit enlarged. The pillars of the crossing gates remained at the time of writing.

At Avonwick there have been additions to the buildings and today the station is used as a 'B&B' whilst Gara Bridge has been extensively altered - almost to beyond recognition. However it is pleasing to know that most of the branch buildings survive.

At Brent all the station buildings were demolished after closure (1964) although the signal box remains on what is left of the island platform. The box serves as a rather luxurious PW cabin. Although fire destroyed part of the goods shed some years ago it is now in industrial use with the yard acting as a car park.

Plans to revive this railway were discussed in the early 1980s by a local group. However these plans were more than rose-tinted. With much of Kingsbridge station area occupied and the housing development where could the housing go? It could only be a pipe dream and soon all hopes and dreams faded and plans were left to gather dust.

It is imperative that anyone wishing to visit or walk along the old railway

The rear of Gara Bridge station 1993. *Dermot Reynolds*

Three-road river bridge just south of Gara Bridge in 1993. *Dermot Reynolds*

Loddiswell station in the 1990s. The station nameboard is now positioned on the former goods shed wall. *Dermot Reynolds*

trackbed must first obtain permission from the new owners as this is largely in private ownership - please do not trespass.

The railway has now long since gone from the South Hams and nature proceeds with its task of reclamation it is becoming progressively more difficult to trace the course of this once idyllic branch - however one can still stand at various locations and let the imagination take over: the distant sound of a whistle mingling with the wildlife chorus, the screech of the wheel flanges on the curved rails, the staccato bark of the locomotive's exhaust as it echoes off the cutting, then, finally, the unforgettable sight of the little green '45XX' tank engine and its two coaches as it sways into view with that characteristic aroma of steam and hot oil - alas only a memory now in this part of 'Glorious Devon'.

A poem written by T.W.E. Roche and given to one of the authors when preservation of the branch seemed to be a reality in 1966 follows.

Into Brent's three-platformed station
Steams the lordly London train
4561 standing patient
Simmering in the moorland rain.

Cream and chocolate Kingsbridge coaches
Are uncoupled and the tank
From the branch line now approaches
By the primrose-covered bank.

Buffers up; a lordly whistle
Plymouthwards the 'Castle' pounds
To a puff more brisk and brittle
Now the overbridge resounds

As the little Kingsbridge puffer
Sets her London coaches back
Bumps against the branch train's buffer
On the bay's adjacent track.

Right away! the green flag flutters
4561's driver tugs
At the chain; one shriek she utters
Then across the points she chugs.

Out again through verdant cutting
Under the A38
Track on river now abutting
See the Aune come down in spate.

Rattle, rumble, roar of river,
Hiss of steam and piston's clank
Round the bend and with a shiver
Through the cutting deep and dank.

Ferns and foxgloves in profusion
Trembling at her passage quick;
Then the vacuum's sharp intrusion
For the stop at Avon Wick.

Cheerful shout from lonely porter
Now at last the sun breaks through
As beside the tumbling water
4561 chugs anew.

Hither, thither through the valley
See the rail and river run
As they flirt continually
Through the woodland with the sun

Till the trees, the line embowering
Reach the very topmost ridge,
Hillsides o'er the lineside towering
Now betoken Gara Bridge.

What a scene of animation!
In the loop the up train waits,
Horse and cart beside the station
Patient at the crossing-gates.

Pill-boxed station-master striding
Towards us past the flower-beds gay
Camping coaches in the siding
In Great Western brave array.

Fourteen signals guard our passing
Now we're chuffing off once more,
Whistling loud for Topsham Crossing
Twinkling o'er the valley's floor.

Loddiswell's single-platformed station
Greets us next around the curves
In its awkward low location
For the hilltop place it serves.

Final climb to Sorley Tunnel
Tiny glimpse of distant sea,
Sparks fly out from lab'ring funnel
Then again she's running free.

Rattling, clanking, hissing, coasting
Round the final set of bends
Into Kingsbridge, proudly boasting
'*This* is where your journey ends.'

'Oh, Glorious Devon!'

Appendix

Extracts from *Rambles in South Devon**

Ramble No. 11
Torcross, Start Point, Prawle Point and Salcombe
11½ Miles

Cheap Day Ticket, Torquay to Kingsbridge, 4s. 3d.; 'bus, Kingsbridge to Torcross, 1s.; and 'bus, Salcombe to Kingsbridge, 1s.

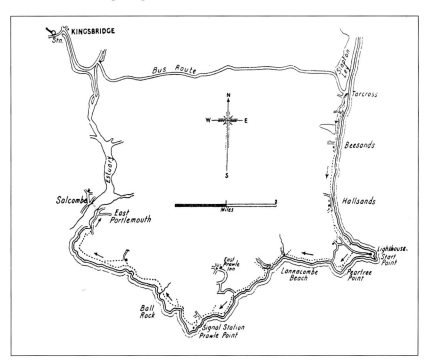

The extreme south coast of Devon provides some of the finest cliff scenery to be found anywhere, an opinion with which those who take this and the following walk can hardly fail to agree. The journey from Torquay is rather longer than for the other rambles, but such splendid walks thoroughly justify it and it is in itself very enjoyable, especially the part down the valley of the Avon, where the single line of railway follows the course of the bubbling little river and several times crosses it.

From Kingsbridge station, take the Dartmouth 'bus to Torcross, alighting at the extreme south end of Slapton Ley, after running along the side of it for half a mile. This freshwater lake, which is well stocked with fish, adjoins the sea for two miles, only being separated from it by a bank of shingle which carries the Dartmouth road, and the close proximity of the fresh and salt water is very peculiar.

* *Railway Rambles in South Devon*, Hugh Page, published by the GWR in 1933.

139

The walk runs right round the coast and, as the path is mostly quite distinct, directions will only be needed in a few doubtful places. Start up some steps on the left of the Torcross Hotel, bear right, then left and keep as near the cliff as practicable. The path presently turns slightly inland and drops precipitously, part of the descent being made by means of an iron ladder, at the foot of which avoid the quarry and bear left towards the beach. Those who do not care about the sharp descent can avoid it by following the main track at first further inland and working round a combe to the beach. Follow the rough track to the right, just above the beach, to Beesands, a natural unspoiled fishing village, where at the Cricket Inn or the shop next door, a mile from Torcross, it will be advisable to have some refreshment, as, apart from the Hallsands Hotel in another mile, there is practically no other opportunity for a further 9½ miles at the end of the ramble.

Continue through the village and at the end bear right up a rough track, but leave it for a forward path when it goes round behind some cottages. On reaching Hallsands Hotel, carry on up, keeping to the upper track later, and at a further private hotel take a left forward footpath, seen along the cliff about halfway up. At a fork, bear up to the right and on the top keep fairly near the cliff, go through a gate ahead and follow the track by a stone wall, taking a path to the right opposite an opening.

Start Point, which has been showing up ahead for some little time, more impressive than imposing, is now fairly close, but unless it is desired to visit the lighthouse, go over the ridge and follow the path to the right, past Peartree Point. On reaching Lannacombe Beach in about a mile, a spread of rocks when the tide is down, keep close to the edge of the cliff and beyond a lane and house, near a shed roofed with an upturned boat, which would have delighted the heart of Dickens, take a right fork. Just beyond a house called 'Crags', turn down to the left at a small direction board, marked 'Footpath', and after crossing a grassy stretch and some cultivated land later cross a lane and continue by the path along the cliff edge.

On coming in sight of Prawle Point, the most southerly point of Devon, surmounted by Lloyd's signal station and recognisable by the natural arch at its base, keep near the sea between the wall and some cornfields; then bear right between the signal station and a row of houses. The coast now becomes more rugged and the imposing Bolt Head comes into sight on the other side of the Salcombe estuary. After a fine two or three miles, avoiding any paths forking definitely inland, Salcombe appears, rising beautifully on its hillside, very similar to Dartmouth, and the path later, after bearing right, runs into a road. Follow this to the left and in about half a mile look out for a track down to the left by a pillar box and a notice board of the 'Haven Tea Rooms'. This leads to the Ferry for Salcombe, where turn right and go up to the church, near which the 'bus for Kingsbridge starts, though if there is time, without risking losing the train there, tea will no doubt be welcome in the town first.

Ramble No. 12.
Kingsbridge, Hope Cove, Bolt Tail, Bolt Head and Salcombe
10½ Miles

Cheap Day Ticket, Torquay to Kingsbridge, 4s. 3d.; 'bus,
Kingsbridge to Milton Lane, 4d.; and 'bus, Salcombe to Kingsbridge, 1s.

Though it is difficult to draw comparisons between different types of scenery, it is probable that the last ramble of this series is the best of all. It is better than No. 11, a similar type of ramble, as practically all the cliff scenery is of the grand and rugged order and nearly all the walk runs along the top, so that the walker gets land as well as sea views

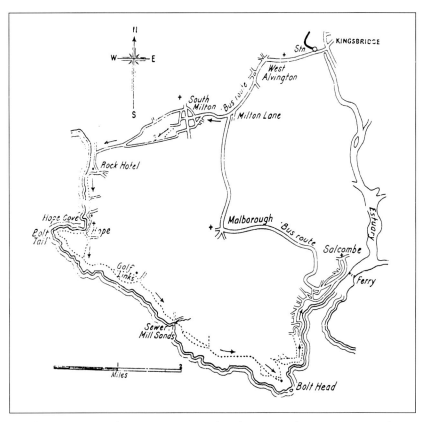

and the full benefit of the breeze. It may be thought by some that Nos. 11 and 12 should have been run in the same direction, so that they could be made continuous if desired, but all the walks have been arranged so that the views can be seen to the best advantage, and the view coming into Salcombe is one not to be missed on either ramble, especially in sunshine, when the sea is a typical Devon or Mediterranean blue. In any case, it would not be difficult to reverse one of the walks, if desired. In these days, when we are threatened with the loss of so many cliff paths, it is gratifying to know that most of this magnificent cliff walk is on National Trust property.

Take the Salcombe or other suitable 'bus from Kingsbridge station and, on alighting at the end of Milton Lane, turn right from the main road. In about half a mile, pass a left turning and presently a cross-road, continuing up a bye-lane, and when it turns left go through a forward gate a little to the right. Cross a short field, continue by a lane, turn left and bear right with it and, where it dips and becomes very muddy, go through a gate on the left and bear left up the field and through another gate. Bear right along a cart-track footpath, through two more arable fields, with a good view on the right of South Milton's unusual fluted church tower and Thurlestone with the sea beyond, to a lane, where bear right. Follow the lane into a road and down to the sandy shore, with the arched Thurlestone Rock opposite, turn left to a road on the left of the Rock Hotel and take the first right turning beyond it to the cliff. There is a fine coast view backward and forward as the path is followed left to Hope Cove, where at the Anchor and Hope Inn, or some of the tea houses in the village, refreshment can be obtained, 3½ miles from the end of Milton Lane.

This quaint little fishing village, very much associated with smuggling in former days, is now becoming popular with visitors who like to take their holidays in natural surroundings. Continue along the road, which keeps fairly near the sea, to the lifeboat house, to the right of which there is a path leading round Bolt Tail for those who do not object to a detour of about a mile. Otherwise, turn left and shortly right into a charming little square, surrounded by typical Devon thatched cottages, though the inevitable galvanised iron is beginning to spoil it, as it is so many other Devon villages.

Continue up past the post office and follow the footpath beyond to the top of the other cliff, where there are further good views backward and forward, and where turn left along the path. Now commences the best part of the walk - improving right on to the end - and the sheer delight of striding over the breeze-swept turf on the top of the rugged red cliffs, their base beaten by the white foamy fringe of the intensely blue sea. No directions are needed until Sewer Mill Sands are reached in well over a mile by dropping sharply slightly inland to a sandy lane, where turn right to the quiet little bathing beach. The various parts of this coast bear some strange and crude names, but this is not really one of them, as the name is simply a corruption of a word meaning seafaring.

Cross two streams and go up the path just beyond the second, past an upright stone which once did service as a gate-post. When the path forks, either the right or left branch can be taken and probably the right will be chosen as being nearer the sea. If so, after passing a group of jagged rocks of fantastic shapes and going through a gap in a stone wall, strike left of a second group of rocks and follow the main path along the cliffs for about a mile. After getting over a stile by a gate, a notice that teas can be obtained at the farm over on the left will be observed. If tea can wait for an hour, take either the path from the stile on the right or the stone stile on the left, as they meet later. If the latter is taken, keep up to the right, with a fine view ahead of Sharp Tor and a triangular patch of sea, which, being visually enclosed by rocky cliffs, looks like a Swiss lake. Where the two paths meet again, unless it is desired to go right to the end of Bolt Head, take the upper path straight over to the path below, where turn left with the telegraph wires down to the old cable hut.

Here there is a choice of two paths, both equally delightful in their own way. One is quite obvious as it passes round Sharp Tor, halfway up the cliff, and later wends its way, with views of Salcombe between the trees, along Courtenay Walk. The other goes over the top, with a much wider and most wonderful view of Salcombe and the Estuary, and necessitates a sharper climb. To accomplish it, just after turning right by the hut take an indistinct left path and, at a leftward bend later, join a more distinct one to the top, the full magnificence of the view opening up on reaching the edge. Follow the path towards Salcombe over several wall stiles, turn right where it joins another and follow the winding track down, joining the lower path at the end of Courtenay Walk.

Turn left round Bolt Head Hotel, right past South Sands, rise and fall with the coast road to North Sands and, just past a left turning and after a sharp rise, a left backward path will be found by a white gate marked 'Sandhills'. A short cut up to the 'bus road can be taken here by following the forward upward road at the end of the path and the steep further path where the road turns sharply right, the main road being at the top and the 'buses stopping at the road junction a little to the right. As, however, at busy times the 'bus may be full there and tea will probably be required in Salcombe, it may be advisable to leave the path alone and continue into the town, returning to Kingsbridge by 'bus, as directed in Ramble No. 11, thus finishing satisfactorily an ideal walk.

Acknowledgements

It seems so inadequate merely to say 'thank you' to the many people the authors have had the pleasure of meeting whilst in the preparation of this work - who have willingly given their time, searched through their personal records, given their continued support, encouragement and hospitality - our very grateful thanks.

We must however acknowledge the invaluable help given over the years by Bryan Gibson - who at one time lived in the Anchor Hotel, Kingsbridge - and David Pattisson for the foreword in our book and reading the completed manuscript making several important revisions.

With actual research taking nearly six years it is impossible to mention all by name who have assisted in one way or another; however we should like to mention specifically the following for information supplied in either verbal, written or photographic form - acknowledgement is also given where appropriate in the text. Also the many photographers who have supplied material who are acknowledged under the photograph.

Wm. Cookworthy Museum, Fore Street, Kingsbridge.
The Devon County Archives,County Hall, Exeter.
The Great Western Society, Didcot, Oxfordshire.
The BR Records Office, London.
The Signalling Record Society
Torbay County Library
Uplands Railway Museum, Bristol.

Ivor Baldwin	Mrs Sheila Hall
Anthony Brindle	Dr R. Holcombe
Miss E. Burgoyne	A. Hunt
Ron Canham	Colin Judge
Mr Chandler	Phillip Kelley
Keith Cooper	Tony Kingdom
Ken Cornelius	Miss Christian Michell
Mr Horace Cox	Arthur Morley
Jack Cox	Mrs Maureen Parsons
John Cummings	Frank Patey
Francis Dean	Tom Patrick
Ray Dunn	Phillip Powell
Len Fairweather	Roy Sambourne
Mr & Mrs Bob Gale	Cecil Talbot
Alan Gidley	H. Wilkinson
Eric Gillard	Dereck Wilson
Percy Hawkes	Bill Wonnacott

No. 4561 is seen here with a Hawksworth 'B' set and an LNER 4-wheel van heading towards Brent c. 1960. *M. Esau*

Bibliography

Acts of Parliament
South Devon Railway, 4th, July, 1844
Kingsbridge & Salcombe Railway (Lord Courtenay 1854 Proposal), 1863
Kingsbridge & Salcombe Railway 27 & 28 Vic. Cap. 287, 29th July, 1864
The South Hams Devon Railway, November 1865
Kingsbridge & Salcombe Railway 29 & 30 Vic. Cap. 264, 23rd July, 1866
Kingsbridge & Salcombe Railway, 1872
Kingsbridge & Salcombe Railway (Narrow Gauge), 1875
Kingsbridge & Salcombe Railway, 24th July, 1882
Kingsbridge & Salcombe Railway, 8th August, 1887
Great Western Railway New Lines Act, 13th August, 1888
The Devon & South Hams Light Railway (Ext. of Totnes Quay Line), February 1900

Minute Books (Railway Companies)
Kingsbridge & Salcombe Railway
The Great Western Railway

Newspapers & Periodicals
The Times, 17th August, 1882
Western Morning News - Various editions
South Devon Times - Various editions
Kingsbridge Gazette - Various editions
Railway Magazine, July 1906
Great Western Railway Magazine - Various editions
Railway Modeller, May 1956
Model Railway Constructor, January 1964
Trains Illustrated, February 1958

Books
History of the Great Western Railway, E. T. McDermot, Ian Allan
West Country Railway History, David St John Thomas, David & Charles
Great Western Coaches, J. H. Russell (Vols. I & II), Oxford Publishing Co.
The Yealmpton Branch, A.R. Kingdom, Oxford Publishing Co.
Go Great Western, T.W.E. Roche, West Country Handbooks
The Land Changed its Face, Grace Bradbeer, David & Charles
The South Hams, Margaret Willy, Robert Hale
Glorious Devon, S.P.B. Mais, GWR
Railway Rambles in South Devon, Hugh Page, GWR
Gone With Regret, G. Behrend, Jersey Artists
Bradshaw's Shareholders Manual - Various editions from 1860
Stock Exchange Year Book - Various editions from 1860